A Short History of the Bahá'í Faith

Dr Peter Smith teaches world history and sociology in the International Students Degree Program (ISDP) at Mahidol University, Thailand.

Books by the same author

The Babi and Baha'i Religions: From Messianic Shi'ism to a World Religion
The Bahá'í Religion: A Short Introduction to its History and Teachings
In Iran: Studies in Babi and Baha'i History (vol. 3)

Other books in this series

A Short History of Buddhism by Edward Conze
A Short History of Judaism by Lavinia and Dan Cohn-Sherbok
A Short History of Islam by William Montgomery Watt

A SHORT
HISTORY
OF THE
BAHÁ'Í FAITH

Peter Smith

ONEWORLD
OXFORD

A SHORT HISTORY OF THE BAHÁ'Í FAITH

Oneworld Publications
(Sales and Editorial)
185 Banbury Road
Oxford OX2 7AR
England

Oneworld Publications
(US Marketing Office)
PO Box 830, 21 Broadway
Rockport, MA 01966
USA

ISBN 1–85168–070–5

Printed and bound by
WSOY, Finland

Contents

PART THREE: THE BAHÁ'Í FAITH SINCE 1922

List of Illustrations

Map

Figure

Tables

Preface

This book provides a short history of the Bahá'í Faith and of the Bábí movement from which it sprang. It is written for those who would like a succinct account of a religion that has become increasingly well known in recent years and has succeeded in gaining a widespread following throughout the world. I have sought to make use of the latest research on the two religions, but have tried to avoid weighting down the text with too many scholarly references. Readers wishing for more detail are referred to my *The Babi and Baha'i Religions* (see references). Inevitably with such a brief work describing complex historical developments, I have had to omit much and to skate over difficult issues. I can only hope that the ice is not too thin.

Undoubtedly, one area that has been neglected is what might be termed the 'faith' dimension of history. For believers, the history of their own religion is more than simply a catalogue of events. Central episodes in particular are invested with mythical and theological meaning that give a colour and texture far different from an academic narrative such as this. Again, I have not included any extended discussion of the wider significance of events or sought to encompass them within some explicit theoretical framework.

Although the Bahá'í Faith grew out of the Bábí movement and its followers regard the Báb as one of the founders of the Bahá'í Faith, the two religions are very different. Rooted in mid-nineteenth-century Iranian Islam, Bábism may seem alien to many modern Western readers; a brief introduction to the

Islamic and Iranian background is therefore provided. For its part, the Bahá'í Faith has clearly undergone an enormous transformation over the 132 years of its existence, most particularly in developing from a movement almost entirely confined to the Middle East into what is effectively a small-scale world religion (now with about five million followers). In the process, it has lost much of its contact with the Islamic and Iranian culture that originally surrounded it. While casual references in the press (and even in some textbooks on comparative religion) may still give the impression that the Bahá'í Faith is an Iranian religion, this is no longer the case. Bahá'ís respect Iran as the land of their religion's birth and regard Islam as part of the process of divine revelation that includes all the major world religions, but they stress the independence of their Faith. Demographically, too, Iranians now comprise only a small minority in a religion whose main centres of growth are in monsoon Asia, sub-Saharan Africa and Latin America.

Moojan Momen and Juan Cole were kind enough to read through the draft of this book. To them my thanks. They are guiltless for the faults that remain. I must also thank Firouz Anaraki for his logistical support, Sammireh Smith for typing parts of the original manuscript and my children for their good-natured endurance of the trials engendered by fathers who write books. Very special thanks must go to Hassan Sabri and to Roger and Muriel Wilkinson for their encouragement, and to them this book is dedicated.

Peter Smith
Bangkok,
July 1995

Part One

THE BÁBÍ RELIGION, 1844–53

The Islamic and Iranian Background

The Bahá'í Faith centres on the person of Bahá'u'lláh (1817–92), its prophet-founder, but to understand its origins, we must examine both the Bábí movement from which it emerged and the complex world of mid-nineteenth-century Iranian Shí'ism in which Bábism is rooted. The Bahá'í Faith has long since developed in ways that make it distinctively different from Islam, but some reference to these Islamic and Iranian roots is essential. Not only did the Bábí religion emerge as a movement within Shí'í Islam, but the Bábís and early Bahá'ís were almost all Iranians who had formerly been Shí'í Muslims; the writings of the Báb (1817–50) – the founder of Bábism – and to a lesser extent those of Bahá'u'lláh are pervaded by Islamic concepts; and many Bábí and Bahá'í practices bear an obvious resemblance to those of Islam.

Resemblance and derivation are not the same as identity, of course, and to describe the Bahá'í Faith as a Muslim sect – as some writers are still inclined to do – is highly misleading, and as inaccurate as describing second-century Christianity as a Jewish sect.

Islam

Those aspects of the Islamic tradition that are replicated most clearly in the Bábí and Bahá'í religions concern the concepts of revelation and holy law. Thus, in all three religions it is believed that God has addressed humanity through a series of divinely appointed messengers – including Abraham, Moses, Jesus and Muhammad – and that divine guidance for the present age is partly enshrined in a body of holy law based on scriptural revelations brought by the latest divine messenger.

It is these same points, however, that most sharply separate the Bábís and Bahá'ís from orthodox Muslims. For Muslims, Muhammad is the 'seal of the prophets' (understood to mean the last) and the Islamic holy law (the *shari'a*) provides the standard for human behaviour until the resurrection (*qiyáma*). For Bábís and Bahá'ís, the resurrection has already come; the Báb and Bahá'u'lláh are divine messengers (Bahá'ís generally use the term 'Manifestation of God' rather than 'prophet', and include Krishna, Zoroaster and the Buddha in their list of Manifestations); and Islamic law has been abrogated and replaced by the successive revelations of the Báb and Bahá'u'lláh as the proper guides for human beings in the contemporary world. These later revelations contain elements reminiscent of Islam, but are at the same time distinctively different (see chapters 3 and 6 for the main elements of Bábí and Bahá'í law).

Twelver Shí'ism

The branch of Islam that formed the primary matrix in which the Bábí and Bahá'í religions developed was Twelver (*Ithná-'Ashariyyá*) Shí'ism, the state religion of Iran since the sixteenth century.

Shí'ism differs from the Sunní Islam of most Muslims in various ways. Central to it is the devotion shown to a series of Imáms (leaders) who were related to the Prophet Muhammad and whom Shí'ís regard as the recipients of divine grace and guidance. A *Shí'í* is a 'partisan' of the Imáms. Various Shí'í sects have developed, each with its own distinctive teachings and list of Imáms. The Twelvers, now the largest of the Shí'í groups, recognize a succession of twelve Imáms, starting with Muhammad's cousin and son-in-law, 'Alí ibn Abí Tálib (d. 661), and continuing through his descendants until Muhammad al-Mahdí, who disappeared mysteriously in the year 873/4 (AH 260).

In the absence of the Imám, Twelver Shí'ism has developed an intense messianic motif. The Twelfth Imám is regarded as hidden from the eyes of the faithful until the end of time, when he will return to vanquish his opponents and establish a kingdom of peace and justice. Messianic beliefs are also found in Sunnism, forming a recurrently active element in popular religion, but receive little official sanction.

Shí'ís regard the writings, sayings and deeds of the Imáms as an additional source of divine guidance to the revelations of the Qur'án and the oral statements and practices (the *hadíth*) attributed to Muhammad. In this they diverge sharply from the Sunnís, for whom only the latter constitute the basis for their path of tradition (*sunna*). Differences in ritual practice, social law and religious beliefs follow from this divergence, including a far greater readiness on the part of some Shí'í thinkers to study gnosticism. One such gnostically inclined group – the Shaykhís – played a key role in the genesis of Bábism.

Institutionally, Twelver Shí'ism also diverges from Sunnism in the role assumed by the religiously learned (the *'ulamá*). This has changed over time, reflecting the varying fortunes of Shí'ism, but since the late seventeenth century the 'ulamá have been able to establish a degree of authority and autonomy from government control unparalleled in Sunní states. The nature of the Islamic revolution in Iran (1979) reflects this development, and the power of the clerical establishment was a major factor in both the expansion and the persecution of the Bábí movement.

Shí'ism also contains a strong popular emphasis on suffering and martyrdom that is not found in Sunnism. This stems from the oppression and persecution that have been part of the historical experience of the Shí'ís as a minority group. The supreme embodiment of this was the killing of 'Alí's son – the Prophet's grandson – Imám Husayn, at the battle of Karbalá in Iraq in 680, an incident that is still commemorated by the Shí'ís with great emotional intensity. For their part the Bábís readily identified with the faithful defenders at Karbalá during their own sufferings, and Bábí and later Bahá'í readiness to suffer martyrdom became a major 'proof' of their mission for some Shí'ís.

Nineteenth-Century Iran

As a modern country, Iran came into being during the sixteenth-century rule of the Safavids (1501–1722), with Shí'ism coming to act as an important force holding the disparate elements of the population together. Following a period of collapse and fragmentation, the Qájár tribe established a new period of unitary dynastic rule in 1794. The dynasty remained nominally in power until 1925.

Delegating considerable power to provincial governors, the Qájárs acted as suzerains over an enormous empire three times the size of France, but with large areas of sparsely populated desert, semi-desert or mountainous terrain. In the towns, urban élites of military personnel, high-ranking 'ulamá, landowners and merchants enjoyed considerable independence, dominating both urban life and the largely powerless and illiterate peasantry of the surrounding hinterland. Elsewhere, tribes of nomadic and semi-nomadic pastoralists came and went generally as they pleased, frequently dominating the settled population.

The state religion was Twelver Shí'ism, yet there was a perceptible tension between the secular powers and the 'ulamá. Possessing their own economic resources from land grants and religious taxes, and with key institutions located outside Iranian control in the Shí'í shrine cities of Iraq (particularly in Najaf and Karbalá, the burial places of the Imáms 'Alí and Husayn respectively), the higher-ranking 'ulamá frequently assumed a major role in urban politics. They also exercised patronage over the lower-ranking 'ulamá, including village mullás and the bevy of students of sacred law and theology. A clearly defined hierarchy amongst the higher 'ulamá had not then fully developed, and individual *mujtahids* (those who were qualified to exercise their own judgement in matters of religious law) functioned relatively independently, guiding their followers and on occasion becoming involved in bitter disputes with their fellows.

Shaykhism

Disputes between mujtahids sometimes followed legal or theological divisions. Such was the case with the emergence of Shaykhism in the early nineteenth century. Originating in the doctrines of an Arab Shí'í teacher, Shaykh Ahmad al-Ahsá'í (1753–1826), Shaykhism gained a wide following in Iran and Iraq, both amongst the 'ulamá and their lay followers. It was opposed by other 'ulamá who considered it dangerously heterodox, and under the leadership of the Shaykh's successor, Sayyid Kázim Rashtí (d. 1844), it increasingly took on a sectarian appearance. Much early Shaykhí literature is highly abstruse, but it seems clear that in addition to an extreme veneration of the Imáms, the Shaykhí leaders promulgated an essentially gnostic interpretation of Islam, in which they themselves occupied a special position as the unveilers of hidden and esoteric knowledge. They may also have taught at least some of their disciples that the resurrection was near. Thus, there was a widespread response to the Báb's declaration among the Shaykhí community.

The Emergence of the Bábí Movement

The Báb

Sayyid 'Alí-Muhammad, the Báb, was born in the southern Iranian city of Shíráz on 20 October 1819, into a family of traders and merchants. His father, Sayyid Muhammad-Ridá, died while the Báb was still a child (c.1826) and he was brought up by his mother, Fátima Bagum, and under the Guardianship of one of her brothers, Hájí Mírzá Sayyid 'Alí. He was an only child. His family claimed descent from the Prophet Muhammad (hence the title *sayyid*).

As a boy, 'Alí-Muhammad attended a local Qur'ánic school for his elementary education as well as receiving commercial training from his family. Then, when he was fifteen, he began work in his uncle's business in the port city of Búshihr, later setting up as an independent merchant.

Several accounts emphasize the boy's extreme piety, and certainly by the time he was living in Búshihr, religious concerns were of primary importance to him. Thus, in about 1841, he felt impelled to close his office and embark on an extended pilgrimage to the Shí'í shrine cities in Iraq, where his fervent devotion attracted some attention, including among individuals who were later to become his disciples. He eventually returned to his home in Shíráz, where in August 1842 he married one of his cousins, Khadíjih. The young couple's only child died in infancy in 1843.

General view of Shíráz

'Alí-Muhammad's extreme piety and asceticism continued to attract attention, and it seems that he now began to gain a special reputation for holiness, some perhaps going so far as to see him as a living saint with miraculous powers. Certainly, by his own account, he now experienced a number of visionary dreams, in one of the most dramatic of which (in April 1844) he saw the severed head of the Imám Husayn, drops of whose blood he drank and whose grace he thus imbibed. He felt as if the spirit of God had 'permeated' and 'taken possession' of his soul (Nabíl 253). He also began to write on religious themes, this being a highly unusual activity for someone who had not received a specialized clerical education.

The Báb's Declaration and Claims

This growing consciousness of divine inspiration culminated in the Báb's declaration of mission in May 1844. Various accounts of this declaration exist, but the key event was the conversion of one of the most prominent and influential of the younger Shaykhís, Mullá Husayn Bushrú'í (c.1813/14–49), which occurred on the evening of 22 May 1844. This represented a turning point. Not only did 'Alí-Muhammad now claim to be the bearer of a divine mission, but he had gained his first disciple. A new religious movement had come into being.

The exact nature of 'Alí-Muhammad's early claims and of the understanding of them within the fledgling Bábí movement remains ambiguous. Eventually, the Báb was to lay open claim to be the awaited Imám – the Mahdí – and to be the bearer of a new divine revelation, but at first he was widely understood to be claiming to be only the intermediary – the *báb* or 'gate' – between the Hidden Twelfth Imám and the Shí'í faithful. Thus he became generally known as the Báb and his followers as Bábís.

Different readings have been made of the *Qayyúmu'l-Asmá'*, the most important of the Báb's early writings and begun on the night of his initial declaration. Terminology suggesting that he was the gate of the Imám was used, but it seems highly likely that more was intended. Thus, the *Qayyúmu'l-Asmá'* itself is composed in the manner of the Qur'án and, although written at the behest of the Hidden Imám, is also presented as 'new verses from God'. Higher claims are implicit: the Báb was the Imám's 'own self in the worlds of command and creation' (MacEoin, 'From Shaykhism to Bábism' 159–60, 173–4), and clerical readers in Karbalá and elsewhere were quick to condemn the book as purporting to be the 'descent' of 'divine revelation'.

Given that the Báb was later to make explicit claims of this nature, it may well be that they were intended from the beginning but were initially concealed. Certainly in 1847 the Báb referred to the progression of his claims, his initial position being intended to prevent people from becoming agitated by the coming of a 'new book' (or revelation) (Amanat 199).

In whatever way the Báb's initial status was understood, it was clear from the beginning he was making extraordinary claims to authority in Shí'í terms. The challenge to the 'ulamá was particularly clear. Even if the Báb was only the Imám's intermediary, he was now to be seen as the supreme authority in the Shí'í world, and the 'ulamá could only continue to exercise their own authority as his agents. His claims demanded a response, whether it be the utter devotion of his followers or the bitter enmity of his opponents.

Apart from the complex nature of the Báb's particular religious claims, his actual appeal as a religious leader was evidently multi-faceted. Thus, his declaration occurred in the context of the crisis in Shaykhi leadership that followed Sayyid Kázim's death in Karbalá (2 January 1844). There was no appointed successor, and several of the leading disciples advanced claims to leadership. For a significant number of Shaykhís, then, the Báb represented a charismatic successor to the first two Shaykhí masters.

Beyond this there was the Báb's popular appeal. Even prior to the declaration of his claims, the Báb was seen as a saintly ascetic and as such was a potential focus of popular piety. Within Shíráz, this appeal appears to have been strengthened after he commenced his mission, and many people who were not Bábís acquired copies of his writings, for some at least because of the sacred power these were assumed to possess. His appeal as a popular holy man resurfaced at other times in his mission.

Far more specific than this was the Báb's announcement of the near advent of the Imám Mahdí. That his own mission commenced in the year AH 1260 (1844), the thousandth anniversary of the original disappearance of the Twelfth Imám in AH 260, readily accorded with this claim, of course, and both accentuated and attracted the millenarian sentiment that was prevalent at the time.

Initial Expansion

Mullá Husayn and a group of other young Shaykhís who had followed him to Shíráz after the death of Sayyid Kázim accepted the Báb and were then sent by him to various parts of Iran to announce his claims, but without as yet divulging his name. A widespread network of Bábí groups soon came into being, mostly amongst the existing Shaykhí communities. A special messenger, Mullá 'Alí Bastámí, was also sent by the Báb to the Shí'í holy cities in Iraq to present the Báb's claims. Again, first addressing himself to the Shaykhís, Mullá 'Alí succeeded in gaining a considerable number of converts, both Iranian and Arab. When he turned to the most prominent non-Shaykhí Shí'í cleric (Shaykh Muhammad Hasan an-Najafí), however, he was denounced as a heretic and the Báb's writings branded as blasphemous.

A coalition of Shí'í 'ulamá in Iraq rapidly formed to oppose Mullá Alí's influence, which continued to spread. In January 1845, Mullá 'Alí was tried by a joint tribunal of Sunní and Shí'í 'ulamá and sent to Istanbul, where he was sentenced to hard labour in the Istanbul dockyards.

The Báb meanwhile journeyed to Mecca for the pilgrimage season, accompanied only by one of his disciples and a servant. He proclaimed his cause but elicited little response. Having received news of Mullá 'Alí's reception in Iraq, he cancelled a projected gathering of his followers in Karbalá, where they were to await the arrival of the Mahdí, and instead returned to Shíráz (July 1845). This change of plan was attributed to *badá'*, the alteration of divine decree in response to changed circumstances, an essentially heretical doctrine, which indicated the unorthodox nature of Bábí millenarianism (Smith, *Bábí and Bahá'í Religions* 16). Some of those who had been caught up in the general millenarian excitement of the Báb's first announcement fell away, leaving only the most committed.

Even before the Báb's arrival in Shíráz, one of his disciples there had openly proclaimed that the Báb was the representative of the Hidden Imám. As in Iraq, there was uproar, and several of

23

the Bábís were brutally punished and expelled from the city, whilst the Báb himself was placed under house arrest on arrival. He was later induced to disclaim publicly that he was the *báb* of the Imám, but in Shí'í terms, this denial was not necessarily significant: it was made under duress and could therefore be accepted as pious dissimulation (*taqiyya*), a traditional Shí'í practice in times of danger. Neither did it prejudice any higher claims that the Báb might wish to make.

Despite these events, the movement continued to spread and remained effectively co-ordinated, with the Báb relaying instructions through his immediate attendants in Shíráz to his disciples in other parts of Iran. He also received some visitors, including Sayyid Yahyá Dárábí ('Vahíd'), a high-ranking cleric with court connections who may have been delegated by the Shah to investigate the Báb's claims, and representatives of Mullá Muhammad-'Alí 'Hujjat' from the city of Zanján. Vahíd and Hujjat became the first important converts from outside the Shaykhí community.

The Báb's disciples were meanwhile establishing Bábí groups in many centres, mostly amongst existing Shaykhí communities, but also more widely, perhaps particularly amongst those already influenced by various forms of Shí'í heterodoxy. In several cities they encountered strong opposition from the leading clerics and their progress was blocked, but over the next few years they gained adherents in most of Iran's major cities as well as more extensively in smaller towns and villages in the northern provinces of Khurásán and Azerbaiján. The disciples' own clerical status was an important factor in attracting converts, and in several instances there was mass conversion of the followers of a particular cleric, most prominently in the case of Hujjat in Zanján, a large proportion of whose inhabitants became Bábís. A similar situation later developed in the southern town of Nayríz through the activities of Vahíd.

Of particular note was the situation that developed in

Karbalá. Bábí leadership there was exercised by one of the Báb's most passionate disciples – and also the only woman among them – Fátimih Baraghání (1814–52), a daughter of a prominent cleric in Qazvín, western Iran. She is known by the titles *Qurratu'l-'Ayn* ('Solace of the Eyes') and *Táhirih* ('the Pure One'), bestowed on her by Sayyid Kázim and the Báb respectively. Whilst other Bábí leaders were generally cautious in their presentation of the Báb's claims and teachings, she was audacious and often provocative, a stance underlined by her implicit rebellion against the restraints of the traditional female role. She was finally arrested by the Ottoman authorities and expelled from Ottoman Iraq to Iran in March 1847.

The Relationship with Shaykhism

As it first developed, the Bábí movement was effectively a subsect within Shaykhism. The Báb's first disciples, as noted, were all Shaykhís and the initial Bábí missionary expansion was concentrated within the existing Shaykhí communities.

For his part, the Báb addressed Shaykhí concerns but was not properly part of the Shaykhí tradition. Some of the Báb's family had been sympathetic to Shaykhism, and the Báb himself was familiar with basic Shaykhí ideas – his writings contain frequent references to Shaykhí themes. However, despite having attended some of Sayyid Kázim's classes in Iraq and later referring to him as 'my teacher', the Báb never made any formal study of Shaykhism. While he shared the Shaykhí tradition of gnostic exposition of scripture, the Báb's approach was distinctively his own. He claimed leadership of the Shaykhís in succession to Sayyid Kázim, but at the same time claimed a status that transcended that of the first two Shaykhí leaders.

The distinctiveness of the conception of the Báb's leadership

as compared to that of the first two Shaykhí leaders is emphasized by the accounts of Mullá Ḥusayn's acceptance of the Báb's
claims. Initially he rejected the Báb on the grounds that he was
not a member of the 'ulamá and hence not competent to make
religious claims (Amanat 169). His subsequent acceptance
therefore marked a major transposition in his understanding of
religious authority, and one that can be traced in other Bábí
conversion accounts.

The Báb's claims were also distinctive in that they represented a powerful assertion of the messianic elements that appear
to have been present in Sayyid Kázim's later teachings. This was
in clear contrast to what was soon to become mainstream
Shaykhí orthodoxy.

While the Báb made a powerful appeal to some Shaykhís –
and active Bábí groups within the existing Shaykhí communities
soon became the foci for more widespread expansion – his claims
and teachings appalled others. The result was a schism, and conse-
quently Shaykhí leaders in both Iraq and Iran became prominent
in condemning the Báb and his followers. They also took pains to
distance themselves from the Bábís, and to de-emphasize the more
heterodox elements of Shaykhí belief. The most important of
these men was Ḥájí Muḥammad Karím Khán (1809/10–70/1),
from the south-eastern city of Kirmán, who assailed the Bábís in
successive writings and consolidated his leadership over the
majority of those Shaykhís who rejected the Báb's call.

Relationships with the 'Ulamá and Secular Authorities

The initial response of the religious and secular authorities to the
Báb and his followers was mixed. For the most part, the 'ulamá
rejected his claims and incited an increasingly violent persecution of his followers. A minority of 'ulamá became believers,

however, either openly or covertly. Although senior clerics (with some prominent exceptions) generally opposed the Bábís, lesser 'ulamá were from the start the backbone of the Báb's movement. Where the Bábí 'ulamá were men of authority and influence, there were widespread conversions amongst their lay followers.

Despite the powerful challenge of the Báb's claims, some 'ulamá reserved judgement, impressed, it would seem, by the Báb's piety and aura of holiness, but thinking him naive and that his reason had been overcome by his own enthusiasm. The attitudes of two of these men, the powerful heads of the 'ulamá in Shíráz and Isfahán, were important factors in protecting the Báb from the enmity of their fellows, many of whom demanded his death.

As far as the government was concerned, a definite policy towards the Bábís was slow to emerge. The chief minister, Hájí Mírzá Áqásí, seems to have opposed the movement at an early date, but he appears to have been constrained by a growing sympathy for the Báb on the part of Muhammad Sháh, itself reflecting the monarch's inclination towards popular religiosity.

The attitudes of local governors varied, determined no doubt as much by their wish to maintain public order and to pacify (or in some cases perhaps to aggravate) the leading local 'ulamá as by their own religious convictions. The ease with which the Bábí missionaries were, at first, able to gain converts differed considerably from place to place.

The Báb's Early Writings and Teachings

The full extent of the Báb's literary output is not known, as many of his writings were later lost or deliberately destroyed as the movement became subject to increasing persecution. It is clear, however, that the Báb lived in 'an atmosphere of revelation' (Muhammad, 'Some new notes on Bábism' 450), and that

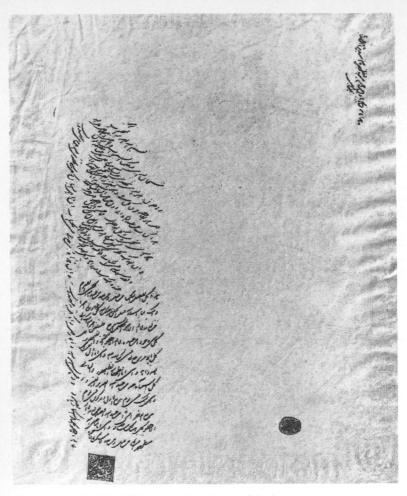

Facsimile of the Báb's Tablet to the first Letter of the Living

'revealing verses' became one of his major activities. Thus by about 1847, the Báb himself estimated that he had revealed some half-million verses (perhaps five million words), of which only 100,000 had been circulated (MacEoin, *The Sources for Early Bábí Doctrine and History* 15). The Qur'án, by comparison, comprises 6,236 verses.

Of the Báb's early writings, several of the most important took the form of commentaries on particular chapters of the Qur'án, but their main purpose was to proclaim the Báb's authority and the arrival of the day of resurrection rather than to provide commentary in any traditional sense. These works included the *Qayyúmu'l-Asmá'*, a commentary on the Qur'ánic Súra of Joseph, which was widely copied by the Bábís and used as a proof-text of the Báb's claims. Other commentaries were written as proofs for eminent 'ulamá.

Other early writings include prayers; answers to doctrinal questions; proclamatory letters to the Shah, his chief minister and to various 'ulamá; and treatises on proper conduct and on aspects of gnostic truth. Many of these writings are in Arabic and abound in esoteric allusions. They would not have been readily accessible to the majority of Iranians, but undoubtedly conveyed an intense religious charge. Indeed, a frequently cited 'proof' of the Báb's mission was his revelation of verses, and the actual act of revelation in which the Báb chanted new divine verses was intensely compelling for his adherents, several of whom were converted in this manner.

Apart from his own claims to authority and the complex esotericism in which they were presented, the Báb's early teachings did not diverge markedly from Islamic orthodoxy. In fact, by insisting on extreme piety and instituting various ascetic practices – extra fasts and prayers – the Báb ensured strictly orthodox practice among his followers.

CHAPTER

3

The Development of a New Religion

The Báb's Changing Fortunes

The Báb's confinement under house arrest in Shíráz ended in September 1846, when he was able to leave the city amidst the confusion caused by an outbreak of cholera. He travelled straight to Isfahán, where he became the guest of the province's powerful governor, Manúchihr Khán. A Christian convert to Islam, Manúchihr Khán is said to have become an ardent supporter of the Báb, taking him under his protection and promising to arrange a meeting with the Shah. Political motivations on the governor's part may also have been involved, of course: a popular holy man could attract political support for his patron.

The 'ulamá of Isfahán were opposed to the Báb and, despite the sympathy of the Friday prayer leader (*Imám Jum'ih*), condemned him as an apostate. In this they gained the support of the Shah's chief minister, Áqásí, an enemy of Manúchihr Khán. Faced with Áqásí's order to send the Báb to Tehran, Manúchihr Khán instead concealed him in his own apartments awaiting events.

The Báb's hopes of gaining the Shah's support were soon dashed. Manúchihr Khán died in February 1847, and the Báb now had no protector; meanwhile, although Muhammad Sháh expressed the wish to meet the Shírází saint, it was his chief minister who determined events. Accordingly, the Báb was brought towards Tehran under armed escort, but then with fresh instructions was taken to the remote prison fortress of Mákú, a place under Áqásí's control near Iran's north-western border with Ottoman Anatolia and Russian Transcaucasia. He remained in Mákú from the summer of 1847 until the spring of 1848.

Áqásí's own antagonism towards the Báb was perhaps at first motivated by the danger that the Bábís were seen to pose to public order by their preaching. Underlying this, however, is likely to have been his fear of the influence the Báb might be able to exert on the Shah. Áqásí's own position relied on his role as the Shah's Sufi master and he was already widely unpopular with other members of the Qájár élite. He did not wish to be displaced.

The Báb's imprisonment in Mákú marked a dramatic change in fortune, and while he continued to petition the Shah, he was now clearly a prisoner of state. Gradually, however, he won the support of his gaoler and elements in the local Kurdish population, and his influence continued to increase, even alarming the Russian ambassador, who was fearful of unrest amongst the Shí'ís of Russian Azerbaiján. Accordingly, in April 1848 the Báb was transferred to the even more remote fortress of Chihríq, where he was placed under stricter confinement. Even under these conditions, however, the Báb was able to communicate with his followers through particular disciples. His public popularity also continued to surge, and many miracles were attributed to him, with even the water from the public bath in one town in which he stayed being taken away by the populace, who believed that it was endowed with sacred power after the Báb had used it.

Tabríz and Badasht

Although Bábism had already emerged as a distinctive and heterodox religious movement, it remained essentially part of Shí'í Islam until the summer of 1848, when the Báb openly announced his claim to be the return of the Imám Mahdí. The implications of this announcement were revolutionary: it marked the era of resurrection (*qiyáma*) and represented a challenge to the entire social order, including both secular and religious authorities.

This 'second declaration' was made first in a letter written towards the end of his imprisonment in Máků (probably early in 1848) and circulated widely amongst the leading Bábís. The declaration was made again in July 1848, when the Báb was brought before a religious tribunal in Tabríz, the capital of Iranian Azerbaiján, this time in the presence of the crown prince who was then governor of the province.

Accounts of the Tabríz trial vary (see Amanat 387–94), but it is clear that the assembled clerics (all Shaykhís) sought to ridicule the Báb, dismissing his claims, and asking him to perform a miracle if he really was the Mahdí. The Báb replied that his proof was the revelation of verses, but the clerics only faulted his grammar. Given the widespread public support for the Báb in the province, the government authorities appear to have tried to defuse the situation. Nevertheless, at the insistence of the Báb's most determined clerical opponents, the Báb was given the bastinado (beaten on the soles of the feet with a cane), no doubt in part to humiliate him. A religious *fatwá* (legal pronouncement) was also issued against him, declaring him an apostate, but granting a reprieve from execution if there was doubt as to his sanity. The Báb was afterwards returned to the prison of Chihríq.

The impact of the Báb's dramatic declaration was reinforced by news of the conference of Badasht (June–July 1848). Accounts of this meeting again vary, but its challenging impact is clear. Held in a remote hamlet in northern Iran, it brought together a number of the leading Bábís and others to discuss plans for future action. In particular it was necessary to work out

The fortress of Máků, near the Turkish and Armenian borders

The castle of Chihríq, near the Turkish and Iraqi borders

the implications of the Báb's claim to mahdíhood and to plan some response to his continuing imprisonment. Two rival positions emerged. One, vehemently proposed by Táhirih, was that the time had now come to abandon constraint, oppose the forces of unbelief and prepare to establish the messianic kingdom of the Mahdí. The Islamic sharí'a was no longer in effect, she said, a point she emphasized by removing the veil from her face and, on one occasion, appearing in men's clothing and on horseback with a drawn sword to urge the other Bábís to action. In all this, she was at first opposed by Mullá Muhammad-'Alí Bárfurúshí, known as Quddús ('Holy'), one of the Báb's closest disciples, who had accompanied him to Mecca. He insisted on continuing constraint and quiet piety, and denounced Táhirih as heretical. By the end of the meeting, however, Quddús had abandoned his opposition and the two were reconciled: a definite radicalization of the movement had occurred.

What was then intended is uncertain. Attacked by villagers on their journey from Badasht at the end of the conference, the Bábís scattered. The events of Badasht had been extremely traumatic for many of them. One man had tried to kill himself at the sight of Táhirih – for the Bábís the embodiment of purity – unveiled. Others had abandoned their faith. Yet others openly broke with Islamic practice, either to 'gratify their selfish desires' (Nabíl 298), or as a deliberate act to proclaim the new day. News and rumours about Badasht soon spread, creating considerable scandal. Many of the Bábís interpreted Táhirih's behaviour as a messianic act, but to others it was an indication of immorality. This was certainly the position taken by Muslim opponents, but even Mullá Husayn, on hearing a report of the conference, apparently threatened to scourge its participants or even to kill them (cited in Balyuzi, *Edward Granville Browne* 75; cf. Amanat 328).

Bábí Law and the Bayán

The Báb's own intentions at this point are indicated by his revelation of the *Bayán* ('Exposition'), his book of laws. Written both in Persian and in a shorter Arabic version, the *Bayán* was a new holy book superseding the Qur'án. The Báb was not simply the Mahdí, but appeared as a new point of revelation. Islamic law had been abrogated, but it was replaced by a new holy law – there was no allowance for the antinomianism that characterized the behaviour of some of the participants at Badasht. Despite the book's obvious importance, it had limited immediate impact on the Bábís. Composed in Mákú (either in late 1847 or the early months of 1848), its length (about 95,000 words) and the increasing difficulties of communication among the Bábís militated against it receiving wide circulation. It stands as an expression of the Báb's own vision of his faith.

As to law, the Báb's system was entirely different from that of Islam, although similar terminology was often employed (Bahá'í law is different again, although it does retain some Bábí elements; see chapter 6). Thus there were distinctive forms of ritual prayer, fasting, pilgrimage and tithing. Pilgrimage, for example, was to be to the Báb's house in Shíráz. Great emphasis was also placed on invocations to God and a general state of prayerfulness. A new solar calendar was introduced consisting of nineteen months of nineteen days, starting on the traditional Iranian new year's day at the spring equinox. A modified form of this is used by Bahá'ís. Extreme cleanliness was stressed, and the Shí'í concern with ritual purity de-emphasized. Marriage was declared to be obligatory and divorce possible only after a year of waiting (the latter is still Bahá'í practice), thus ending the possibility of a husband instantly divorcing his wife, then common practice in Iran. Limited conversation between (unmarried) men and women was permitted. Gentleness was commended and all were to avoid causing sorrow to others. Teachers and parents were not to beat children severely. Animals were to be treated kindly and not overworked. The use of tobacco, opium and alcohol was forbidden, as was the study of grammar, logic, scholastic philosophy and unprofitable sciences. The study of talismans was recommended and instructions given regarding their manufacture. The bodies of the dead were to be treated with great respect and buried in coffins of stone or crystal. Iran was to become a Bábí state, and future Bábí kings were commanded to expel unbelievers (that is, non-Bábís) from their lands, unless they were engaged in useful professions. Non-Bábí books were to be destroyed. Nonbelievers were to be treated with justice and not converted forcibly, but intermarriage with them was forbidden.

Economic reforms were also advocated. There was to be a stable monetary system with a specified value of gold and silver, and merchants were allowed to charge interest (in contrast to Islamic law). Mercantile correspondence was to be inviolate – the efficiency of western posts and communications was praised and recommended for emulation.

Apart from these laws, which are interspersed throughout the book, the *Bayán* contains statements of Bábí doctrine (see below), including explanations of various Islamic eschatological terms.

Later Bábí Doctrine

During his years in Mákú and Chihríq, the Báb wrote extensively. Apart from the *Bayán*, he composed several other books which dealt with aspects of Bábí doctrine. He also completed nine commentaries on the whole Qur'án, a discussion of the 'science of talismans' and numerous prayers.

Although still employing Shí'í and particularly Shaykhí terminology and concepts, these later writings indicate that, as well
as superseding Islamic law, the Báb was also now presenting a
new religious framework distinct from that of Islam. There was a
clear contrast with his earlier writings, which were written within
an Islamic paradigm, and in which heterodox ideas were likely to
be concealed in esoteric language.

What is of particular note is a new doctrine of eschatological promise: the coming of 'He whom God shall make manifest'
(*Man-yuzhiruhu'lláh*). This personage would be the origin of all
divine names and attributes, and all were to seek refuge in him.
Not to believe in him would be to cease being a believer. A thousand perusals of the *Bayán* would not be equal to reading one of
his verses. He would arise suddenly at a time known only to
God, and no one would be able to advance such a claim falsely.
In the meantime, all were to rise on hearing his name and in
every meeting a vacant place was to be left for him.

Central to the theology of the Báb's system, as also in Bahá'í
belief, was the concept of the Manifestation of God (*mazhar-i
iláhí*). This doctrine holds that God is in essence unknowable and
inaccessible. The purpose of human creation is the knowledge
and love of God, but this is only possible through the
Manifestations of God. These beings originate from the Primal
Will or Logos. They combine the station of revelatory divinity
with human servitude. There is a succession of Manifestations,
starting with Adam and continuing through Muhammad to the
Báb and in the future to 'He whom God shall make manifest', and
so on indefinitely. Each is the rising and setting of the same sun,
but each gives a more comprehensive and developed expression
of the divine teachings, encompassing all previous
Manifestations.

Each appearance of a Manifestation of God represents a

re-enactment or return (*raj'a*). The Manifestation appears in obscurity and suffers persecution until eventually his dispensation develops and triumphs. Around him circle his chief disciples, and opposing him are the forces of negation, headed by the Dajjál or antichrist. He is preceded by forerunners, who prepare humanity for the new dispensation at a time when the light of its predecessor has grown dim. Thus the Báb's first disciples, the Letters of the Living, were identified with the holy ones of Shí'ism (Muḥammad, Fátima, the Twelve Imáms and the four Gates), Karím Khán Kirmání was the one-eyed antichrist of prophecy and Ḥájí Mírzá Áqásí was his hideous companion, the Sufyání. Shaykh Aḥmad and Sayyid Kázim were the Báb's heralds. Whether these figures were to be seen as archetypal players in a dispensational drama (as is the case with the Bahá'í interpretation of this doctrine) or actual re-embodiments of former personages (as some Bábís apparently believed) is unclear.

According to the Báb, prophetic fulfilment was a spiritual reality. The events recorded in Shí'ite eschatology had all come to pass, but as spiritual rather than physical events. Those who believed in the Manifestation of God for the present age had attained paradise, and those who had met him had met God. Those who denied him were already in hell fire. Each believer in the former dispensation thus faced the final judgement in terms of his response to the present Manifestation. There was no resurrection of the body.

As in his earlier writings, the Báb continued to make great use of esoteric symbolism, in particular numerology, whereby the underlying structure of the universe could be described. The number nineteen (equivalent to the words *wáḥid*, unity, and *wujúd*, God's absolute being) was greatly emphasized, and alchemical and colour symbolism was also employed.

Conflict and Collapse, 1848–53

The Radicalization of Bábism

There is an evident contrast between the first few years of the
Bábí movement's development and its emergence as an essentially new religion in 1848. The theological focus of this
change was the Báb's advancement of his higher claims, but this
represented only part of a general 'radicalization' of the movement. Other aspects of this process were changes in internal
Bábí organization, the interactive growth of anti-Bábí and Bábí
militancy, and the Báb's own alienation from the Qájár regime.

With the Báb isolated in Mákú and Chihríq, contact
between him and his followers became more difficult.
Communications were maintained, but the leading disciples
increasingly played a dominant role in the direction of the
movement – the holding of the Badasht conference represents
an element of this. This situation received theological legitimacy
from the doctrine that the Letters of the Living represented the
return (*raj'a*) of the holy figures of Shí'ism, and more particularly
from the charismatic authority accorded to the three leading disciples – Mullá Husayn, Táhirih, and Quddús – who came to be
seen as expressing aspects of the Báb's messianic role. Of the
three, Mullá Husayn was formally accorded the position of the
Báb's deputy (*Bábu'l-Báb*), but eventually it was Quddús who
came to be regarded as a second point of revelation to the Báb.

Militancy was always implicit in the Bábí movement in so far as it expressed traditional Islamic messianic expectations, according to which the Mahdí would lead the faithful in a holy war (*jihád*) to establish his kingdom of justice. The theoretical position here was quite complex. In his early writings, the Báb, speaking as or for the Mahdí, referred to the approaching jihád. In the event, however, the jihád was never called and the Báb instead directed his disciples to promulgate his message peacefully, whilst he himself sought to gain the allegiance of the Shah. Later doctrine was different: according to the *Bayán*, it would be future Bábí kings who would lead the jihád.

Again, this messianic charge, with its implications of militancy, was combined with the pietism and the complex esotericism of the Báb's teachings: the Bábís were never simple millenarians. There were also differences of approach among the Bábís, some evidently being more inclined towards militancy than others. The confrontation between Táhirih and Quddús at Badasht reflected these differences.

The context of events was also crucial. The growth of more militant attitudes was interactive; as clerical opposition to the Bábís increased, so too did the occurrence of violent, clerically inspired assaults on Bábí missionaries. Initially, these attacks were not resisted by the Bábís, but they are likely to have contributed to a hardening of Bábí attitudes towards their opponents, which in turn made resistance more likely, whilst the carrying of weapons for defence increased the potential for violent confrontation. As the Bábí movement expanded, and particularly as it made significant inroads into particular urban populations, it necessarily entered into the complex and frequently violent networks of communal rivalries and partisan politics, in which religious differences might exacerbate existing antagonisms. This had already occurred in the case of Shaykhism. It also happened at a personal level, where the previous relationships between individual prominent Bábís and others had a bearing on their roles as Bábís.

These points are relevant to the events in Táhirih's home city of Qazvín in 1847, which served to define the hostility between the opponents of Bábism and the Bábís. The religious situation in Qazvín was already tense when Táhirih returned to the city at her family's insistence in the summer of 1847. The dominant cleric in the city was her uncle and father-in-law, Hájí Mullá Muhammad-Taqí Baraghání, who was already a fierce and powerful opponent of Shaykhism. Táhirih's expulsion from Iraq (March 1847) had not lessened her fervour and in her home city she both proclaimed the Báb's cause and openly broke with her orthodox Shí'í husband, regarding him as an unbeliever. These actions further antagonized her uncle, who was unable to tolerate yet further heterodoxy. There was increasing tension between the two parties, and violent attacks were made on the Bábís; Muhammad-Taqí was then murdered by a Shaykhí with Bábí sympathies. Although denying complicity, the Qazvín Bábís as a group were blamed for the murder, and extensive persecution began, with several of the Bábís being killed. Throughout Iran, the clerical view of Bábism as a dangerous heresy was reinforced by these events, while many Bábís became increasingly assertive and militant in their attitudes.

The final element in the radicalization of Bábism was the Báb's changing attitude towards the Qájár regime. It was only after the Tabríz trial that he seemed finally to abandon hope that Muhammad Sháh would eventually come to his assistance. The implications of this change are evident in the denunciatory letters that he addressed to the Shah and his chief minister after the trial. In these 'Sermons of Wrath' Áqásí was cursed and condemned as an apostate and as 'Satan'. The Shah, too, was reproved for his actions towards the Báb and warned that there remained but little time for him to make amends. Those who opposed the Báb were consigned to hell.

The Beginnings of Conflict: Ṭabarsí

The likelihood of conflict between the Bábís and their opponents had greatly increased by the summer of 1848. The Bábís were now well established in many parts of Iran and their messianic expectations had been heightened by the Báb's declaration of mahdíhood. Clerical attitudes were now generally hostile and the Bábís became increasingly beleaguered. Within the movement, a spirit of militancy was replacing earlier caution.

The climax to these developments came in July 1848, when Mullá Ḥusayn, on the Báb's instructions, raised the 'Black Standard', which proclaimed the advent of the Mahdí. From the north-eastern province of Khurásán, he proceeded westward with a growing body of several hundred armed followers. The intentions of Mullá Ḥusayn and his companions remain a subject of speculation. Later Muslim writers were in no doubt that the Bábís' march from Khurásán was a consciously revolutionary act, but to discuss it in purely political terms is undoubtedly misleading. The desire to establish a messianic kingdom was obviously a political objective, but the Bábís' actions suggest religious fervour, not political calculation. Bahá'í accounts, by contrast, state that Mullá Ḥusayn's purpose was simply to assist Quddús, then under house arrest in the Caspian province of Mázandarán, but this leaves unanswered the exact nature of the proposed assistance. Certainly, it would have involved securing Quddús' release from captivity, but then what? The Bábís' over-all plan of action remains unclear.

One possibility is to see the march as a messianic

proclamation, with the Bábís possibly anticipating a widespread popular movement in support of the Báb, and the subsequent establishment of a Bábí kingdom. The carrying of swords, in this context, had a symbolic significance as well as defensive value in conditions of increasing civil disorder. Beyond this, the Bábís may also have thought of marching on to Mákú to secure the Báb's release, by force if necessary, but this is only conjectural.

In the event, the Bábís became mired in conflict. After several months in which the government had seemed close to collapse, Muhammad Sháh died in September 1848. For a time, the complete breakdown of the country into civil war seemed likely, and the crown prince was rushed from Tabríz to take the throne. In this confused situation, the Bábís tried to enter Quddús' home city of Bárfurúsh near the Caspian Sea, but were attacked and several of their number slain. Retaliating forcefully, they repulsed their opponents, killing many. They then withdrew to the small shrine of Shaykh Tabarsí, which they fortified. Other Bábís joined them until their numbers reached perhaps 500 or 600 men. Enduring a seven-month siege (October 1848 to May 1849), the defenders of Tabarsí withstood repeated attacks by first local and then central government forces. Their sacrificial dedication often terrified their opponents, enabling them to withstand greatly superior numbers, but finally, worn down by starvation and cannon fire, they responded to the false offer of a truce and were massacred.

As with the march, the Bábís' struggle at Tabarsí should be seen primarily in terms of religious motivations. The defenders' zeal was sustained by religious dedication and their sense of identity with the sacrificial sufferings borne by the companions of the Imám Husayn. Like them, they might die as martyrs, but their deaths would witness to God's truth, as would their struggle against the forces of unbelief. This was a re-enactment of the

passion drama of Karbalá, a mighty proof of the truth of the
Báb's call for all true Shí'ís.

The Events of 1850

Stunning as the events of Tabarsí were – and many of the Bábís'
opponents also interpreted the struggle as a new Karbalá – the
conflict itself represented a massive blow to the Bábís' logistical
strength. Many Bábí leaders, including Mullá Husayn and
Quddús and several others of the Letters of the Living, had
been killed during or immediately after the conflict, and so too
had many of the most active of the rank and file. A period of
quiescence followed, and it seems likely that many of the Bábís
– including the Báb himself – were in a state of shock at the
extent of their losses. Effective co-ordination of the movement
undoubtedly became more difficult.

Thus it was not until the early months of 1850 that there
were again signs of Bábí activity. There were confused disturbances
in the southern city of Yazd following Vahíd's proclamation of the
Báb's call there, and in Tehran seven eminent Bábís were arrested
and executed, including the Báb's uncle, who had been his
guardian. This latter episode was probably an attempt by the
new government – led by the forceful Mírzá Taqí Khán as chief
minister to the youthful Násiri'd-Dín Sháh – to intimidate the
Bábís in the capital, allegations of a Bábí conspiracy against the
government notwithstanding.

There was then a further lull until May, when two
upheavals began: in the northern city of Zanján and the southern
town of Nayríz. In both cases there were exceptionally large
local concentrations of Bábís led by a local notable: Hujjat and
Vahíd, respectively. Local tensions and rivalries seem to have
been involved in generating conflict between the Bábís and their

opponents, with a rapid escalation of events leading to what were in effect urban civil wars. Once fighting commenced, the Bábís were at first able to defy local and government forces with a fervour that was daunting to their opponents, but they were then worn down by their enemy's superiority in weaponry, eventually accepting the pledge of a truce to end the fighting. As at Tabarsí, the government forces broke their solemn pledge and massacred or enslaved the Bábí survivors.

Of the two struggles, that at Nayríz (initially with 1,500 Bábís, almost half the town's population) was the shorter, ending within a month. At Zanján (with 3,000 Bábís in a city of 20,000 inhabitants), by contrast, the conflict continued for eight months, until January 1851. Zanján was also notable for the presence of women among the Bábí combatants, and the establishment of local government structures by the local Bábí leadership, including the issuing of coinage.

Faced with this fresh evidence of the power of the Bábís, Mírzá Taqí Khán determined to deprive the movement of its central focus and inspiration. In opposition to the views of other members of the Qájár élite, he ordered the execution of the Báb. Accordingly, the Báb was again brought to Tabríz and, on 8 or 9 July 1850, shot in front of a large crowd of onlookers. The event was remarkable; an entire regiment of soldiers faced the Báb and one of his disciples, who were tied together and suspended from a wall. A first regiment of Armenian Christians presumably aimed to miss, reluctant no doubt to shed the blood of a holy man, and the Báb and his companion were unscathed. A second (Muslim) regiment was then summoned, and they completed the task. The strangeness of these events ensured that even in death, the Báb's aura of holiness was preserved. Cast into a ditch, the bodies of the Báb and his disciple were later carried away by one of the Bábís.

Collapse

After the events of 1850 and the final extinction of the Bábí resistance at Zanján in January 1851, there was then a further lull. Our knowledge of what the Bábís were actually doing during this time is extremely sketchy. The nominal leader of the movement following the Báb's execution was Mírzá Yahyá Núrí (c.1832–1912), now better known by his title Subh-i Azal ('Morn of Eternity'). The nature of his position is open to dispute and subject to conflicting retrospective interpretations by his own followers and those of his elder half-brother, Bahá'u'lláh. Although appointed by the Báb to act as leader after him, it seems that he was little more than a figurehead. Certainly, he was young (still in his teens), inexperienced and reclusive, and was unable to maintain the dynamism or cohesion of the Bábís. Indeed, with their founder and most of their leaders now dead, and faced with the continuing threat of persecution by both the religious and secular authorities, the Bábís led a secret and shadowy existence. Many, no doubt, distanced themselves from the movement, or abandoned it altogether. The active remnant divided into different factions, often centring on the claims made to some new spiritual authority by certain Bábís. Doctrinal speculation was rife.

The final blow, which transformed this state of increasing chaos into one of total collapse, occurred in 1852. In Tehran, one Bábí group had determined on revenge for their martyred founder. No doubt they saw the hand of God in the disgrace and subsequent murder of Taqí Khán at the Shah's instructions (January 1852), and wished to punish his master in a similar way. So in August of that year, individuals associated with this group made a bungled attempt on the Shah's life.

Although this was the work of only a small group, all the

Bábís in Tehran now became suspect. All those who could be found were arrested, and in many cases they were tortured to death in various revolting ways. Among those killed who were not involved in the plot was Táhirih. Although there was a resurgence of fighting in Nayríz the following year, the Bábí religion had to all intents and purposes collapsed, its roots torn up by its opponents. That it was to re-emerge, eventually transformed into the Bahá'í Faith, was due almost entirely to the activities of Bahá'u'lláh.

Part Two

THE ESTABLISHMENT OF THE BAHÁ'Í FAITH

Bahá'u'lláh

Bahá'u'lláh ('The Splendour' or 'Glory of God') was the religious title of Mírzá Husayn-'Alí Núrí (1817–92). The son of a landowning notable and former courtier and provincial governor, Mírzá 'Abbás, known as Mírzá Buzurg Núrí (d. 1839), Husayn-'Alí was one of the most socially prominent of the Bábís. Converting in 1844, he was able to use his wealth and social position to provide support and protection to his co-religionists, becoming one of the few non-clerics to occupy a position of importance and authority within the movement.

Bahá'u'lláh and the Revival of Bábism, 1853–66

After the Báb's execution, Bahá'u'lláh's younger half-brother, Subh-i Azal, went into hiding and was unable to maintain the unity of the Bábís. A variety of claimants to supreme authority then emerged, based on the expected appearance of a further messianic figure after the Báb.

Although he opposed the plottings of the more militant Bábís, Husayn-'Alí was one of those arrested in the aftermath of the attempt on the Shah's life. For four months he was imprisoned, under dreadful conditions, with other Bábís in the underground prison in Tehran called the 'Black Pit' (*Síyáh-Chál*). Here, according to his own later account, he experienced initiatory visions. For much of the time the heavy weight of his chains and the awful

Mírzá Buzurg-i-Núrí, father of Bahá'u'lláh

stench of the place kept him awake, but when he did sleep, he felt that a torrent flowed down from his head over his body and every limb was set afire. He then 'recited what no man could bear to hear'. He also saw a sweet-voiced heavenly maiden, who informed all in creation that he was the 'Beauty of God' and the power of His sovereignty. A voice assured him that God would render him victorious (Shoghi Effendi, *God Passes By* 101–2).

Through the efforts of powerful relatives and friends, Bahá'u'lláh's release was eventually secured. Deprived of his property and refusing an offer of asylum in Russia, he was then exiled from Iranian territory. He went to Baghdad in Ottoman Iraq, arriving there in April 1853. What happened next is interpreted differently by the followers of Bahá'u'lláh (the Bahá'ís) and those of Subh-i Azal (the Azalís). What seems certain is that Bahá'u'lláh now began to eclipse Azal as a leader, and that the latter increasingly resented this but insisted on remaining hidden from most of the Bábís for his own protection. Distressed by the resultant tensions, Bahá'u'lláh withdrew from Baghdad in April 1854, preferring to live a more or less solitary life as a dervish for two years in the mountains of Kurdistán. While there he came into contact with local Sufi leaders, however, and rumours of his whereabouts began to trickle back to his family, who begged him to return. He arrived back in Baghdad in March 1856 and was very quickly recognized as the pre-eminent Bábí leader, both by the Bábís and by the Iranian and Ottoman authorities.

During the next seven years, Bahá'u'lláh worked to reinvigorate the Bábí movement in Iran. Living under the relative safety of Ottoman control, Bahá'u'lláh was able to receive Bábí visitors from Iran and encourage the various Bábí groups through an increasing correspondence. He also attracted a band of dedicated personal disciples and wrote several books that had a major and widespread appeal for the Bábís. Chief among these were *The Hidden Words* (*Kalimát-i-Maknúnih*, c.1858) and *The Book of Certitude* (*Kitáb-i-Íqán*, 1862). These books emphasized the importance of the 'spiritual path', outlined the practical, ethical and religious goals of this path, and in the *Íqán* provided the Bábís with a clear account of their religious doctrines, particularly the concept of a succession of Manifestations of God and the fulfilment of prophecy.

Unlike the writings of the Báb, most of the writings of Bahá'u'lláh were readily accessible to ordinary literate Iranians, a factor that may have contributed to the growing leadership role taken by non-clerics in the Bábí movement. Bahá'u'lláh also addressed new themes – notably the concerns of Islamic mysticism (Sufism), as in his book *The Seven Valleys* – and made reference to biblical themes, including prophecy. Some of his other writings were more esoteric, however, including ecstatic poetry that

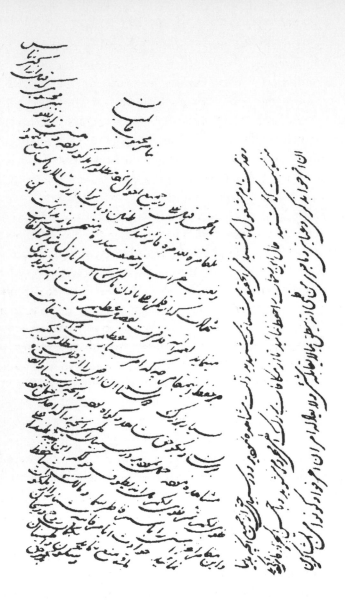

An example of Bahá'u'lláh's own handwriting

referred to his continuing mystical experiences.

Outside the Bábí community, Bahá'u'lláh gained increasing sympathy from both residents and visitors in Baghdad, including Ottoman officials, Iranian notables, and even Sunní and Shí'í clerics. He was widely regarded as an important personage. Faced with the revival of Bábism, the Iranian government sought to have Bahá'u'lláh expelled from Ottoman territory and returned to Iran. This the Ottoman authorities refused to do, instead inviting Bahá'u'lláh – now an Ottoman citizen – to come to Istanbul. He left Baghdad in May 1863 with a number of his disciples. It seems plausible that the authorities may have entertained the hope that the Bábís might be useful to some political purpose, but any such hope was soon dashed. On arriving in the capital in August, Bahá'u'lláh refused to make any political contacts and remained aloof from government ministers. This attitude, combined with further representations from the Iranian ambassador, brought about a marked change in Ottoman dealings with the Bábís, and in December 1863 Bahá'u'lláh and his extensive entourage were exiled to Edirne (Adrianople) in what is now European Turkey.

The Emergence of the Bahá'í Faith

The period of Bahá'u'lláh's exile in Edirne (December 1863 to August 1868) witnessed the final break between Bahá'u'lláh and his half-brother, and thereafter the development of the Bahá'í Faith as a separate religion from Bábism. Concealing his identity from most of the other Bábís, Azal had joined Bahá'u'lláh's entourage on the journey from Baghdad. In Edirne, tensions rapidly mounted, the Bahá'ís accusing Azal of trying to murder Bahá'u'lláh. In 1866, at Bahá'u'lláh's direction, the Bábí colony split between the respective followers of the two brothers, most

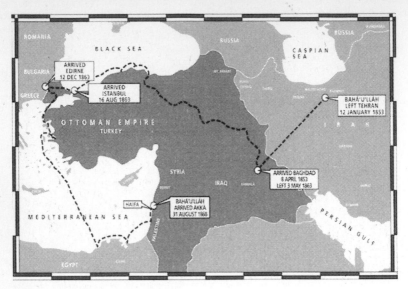

The route of Bahá'u'lláh's exile

siding with Bahá'u'lláh.

Already, in Baghdad, Bahá'u'lláh had gained the fervent devotion of a number of the Bábís, and on the eve of his departure from that city had announced a claim to spiritual authority to at least some of them. This announcement was made in the Garden of 'Ridván' (Rezván, 'Paradise') between 22 April and 3 May 1863, an event later commemorated by Bahá'ís as marking the inauguration of his ministry. In Edirne, Bahá'u'lláh's claims were made generally known and messengers were sent to Iran to communicate them to the Bábís there. Within a few years, the great majority of Bábís had become Bahá'ís, accepting Bahá'u'lláh as the messianic figure of *Man-yuzhiruhu'lláh* ('He whom God shall make manifest') foretold by the Báb. Of those Bábís who did not accept these claims, some identified themselves as Azalí Bábís, while others remained unaffiliated with either group.

In his subsequent writings, Bahá'u'lláh was to establish the

An aerial view of 'Akká, showing the prison in the foreground

A view of the prison in 'Akká, c.1921

laws and teachings of a new religion, but one theme had already emerged by the Edirne period, which served to distinguish the Bahá'ís both from the original Bábís and the Azalís, and this was Bahá'u'lláh's strong emphasis on political quietism: the Bahá'ís were to eschew militancy and be loyal to established governments. The Azalís, by contrast, continued the traditions of religio-political action. Azal himself had been closely involved in the plot to assassinate the Shah, and some of his followers were to play a leading role in the political opposition movements that developed in late nineteenth-century Iran.

The 'Akká Period

The rivalries between the Bahá'ís and the Azalís did not escape the notice of the Ottoman authorities. The Azalís made accusations that the Bahá'ís were plotting sedition, and while a subsequent official enquiry dismissed this charge, it concluded that both Bahá'u'lláh's and Subh-i Azal's religious claims were a potential source of disorder. Aware of the steady flow of Iranian Bábí–Bahá'í visitors, the authorities determined to impose a further banishment on the exiles. Accordingly, in August 1868, Bahá'u'lláh, his family and followers were dispatched to 'Akká – the old crusader city of St Jean d'Acre – in Ottoman Syria, whilst Azal and a few followers were sent to Famagusta in Cyprus. The 'Akká group initially totalled sixty-seven persons: Bahá'u'lláh, two of his brothers, their wives and children, some other relatives, attendants and Bahá'ís. The Ottoman authorities also included two of Azal's followers in the group to act as unofficial spies.

For the next nine years Bahá'u'lláh lived in 'Akká, at first in the fortress and then under confinement in a house in the city. The exiles initially encountered great hostility from the people

An early photograph of Bahá'u'lláh's mansion at Bahjí

of 'Akká and suffered from the severities of their confinement, three growing sick and dying. One of Bahá'u'lláh's sons (Mírzá Mihdí, the 'Purest Branch') died in an accident, an event that was given sacrificial meaning by his father. Endless difficulties were also created by the resident Azalís, and a small group of Bahá'í hotheads eventually murdered them, much to Bahá'u'lláh's distress. Despite these difficulties, communications with the growing Bahá'í community in Iran were re-established, and Bahá'u'lláh even dispatched a messenger to present his claims to Násiri'd-Dín Sháh (the messenger was tortured and then killed). The attitude of the local officials and others became increasingly sympathetic, with even the local muftí becoming devoted to Bahá'u'lláh.

By 1877, the local authorities in 'Akká had become so tolerant of the Bahá'ís that the order of confinement was effectively a dead letter. Bahá'u'lláh was now allowed to move outside the city, eventually settling in the mansion of Bahjí, where he died on 29 May 1892. It was during this lengthy final period of his life that the distinctive features of the Bahá'í Faith as a religious movement were developed. With much of the practical management of the movement in the hands of his eldest son, 'Abbás (1844–1921) – later better known by his title, *'Abdu'l-Bahá* (the 'Servant of Bahá') – Bahá'u'lláh was able to spend much of his time in 'the revelation of verses' and in the enjoyment of nature.

As noted by the English orientalist Edward Granville Browne, who himself visited Bahjí in 1890, Bahá'u'lláh was now 'the object of a devotion and love' from his followers 'which kings might envy and emperors sigh for in vain'. Browne was powerfully affected by his meeting with him, describing Bahá'u'lláh as 'a wondrous and venerable figure', whose face he could neither describe nor forget, and whose piercing eyes 'seemed to read one's very soul'. Though his face was deeply lined with age (he was seventy-two), his 'ample brow' emanated power and authority. He wore both his hair and beard long (the beard almost to his waist) and evidently dyed them jet-black, his hair having turned white after the poisoning attempt by Azal in Edirne. In addition to his robes, he wore a tall dervish hat round the base of which was wound a small white turban (Browne, quoted in 'Abdu'l-Bahá, *Traveller's Narrative*, vol. II, xxxix–xl).

Two years later Bahá'u'lláh died of a fever. In his writings, he had stated that there would be no further Manifestation of God for at least a thousand years, and that the Bahá'ís should not be distressed by his passing: this cause was God's, and his sons would be his successors, and after them the 'Universal House of Justice'. He had also already indicated the primacy of his eldest son, 'Abdu'l-Bahá, and this he emphasized again in his will, directly appointing him his successor and naming his second son, Mírzá Muhammad-'Alí, after him. He also badethe Bahá'ís to maintain their unity and

Entrance to the shrine of Bahá'u'lláh

directed them to abide by his book of laws, the *Kitáb-i-Aqdas* (see chapter 6).

The Growth of the Bahá'í Community

With the establishment of Bahá'u'lláh's leadership of the Bábí–Bahá'í movement in Edirne, processes of consolidation and expansion were set in train. Although an exile, and in 'Akká also a prisoner, Bahá'u'lláh was able to maintain regular contact with his followers in Iran. Bahá'í couriers smuggled letters back and forth, while an increasing number of Iranians, both Bahá'ís and those who wished to investigate Bahá'u'lláh's claims, braved the lengthy and arduous journey to visit 'Akká. Bahá'í agents were appointed at various places along the route to aid these pilgrims. Meanwhile, in Iran, a rudimentary system of Bahá'í organization and leadership was established. In particular, certain outstanding Bahá'ís were appointed by Bahá'u'lláh as 'Hands of the Cause of God' and charged with the co-ordination of the religion within the country.

One regular theme in Bahá'u'lláh's now prolific writings was the necessity of 'teaching the Cause'. Within Iran, Bahá'í missionary teachers accordingly oversaw a cautious but extensive campaign of expansion, and this was later extended to the neighbouring territories of Russian Turkistan and British India. Bahá'í teaching endeavours were also directed towards Iran's Jewish and Zoroastrian minorities, significant numbers of whom converted. Elsewhere in the Middle East, small groups of expatriate Iranian Bahá'ís established themselves in various parts of the Ottoman Empire and in Egypt. There were also a few conversions of Sunní Muslims and Levantine Christians (see chapter 8).

These developments indicated the missionary energy of the Bahá'í religion, and also something of the potential universality of its appeal. This is an important point. Although the Báb had referred to the eventual expansion of his religion to the West, his whole religious system had remained embedded in the world of traditional Iranian Shí'ism. Bahá'u'lláh, by contrast, displayed in his writings an evident sympathy and concern for the followers of pre-Islamic religions, together with familiarity with biblical themes, both of which were unusual for a man of his background. He clearly intended the proclamation of his mission to extend beyond the Bábí and Shí'í milieu.

Expansion also brought a renewal of persecution. Compared to the large-scale massacres of Bábís in the past, this was relatively limited in extent, but it still led to the murder and imprisonment of a considerable number of Bahá'ís in Iran. Unlike the Bábís, however, the Bahá'ís did not resort to militant action, even in their own defence.

CHAPTER

6

The Writings and Teachings of Bahá'u'lláh

Like the Báb, Bahá'u'lláh wrote profusely, particularly during his time in Edirne, 'Akká and Bahjí. With the acceptance of his claim to be a Manifestation of God, all his writings assumed the status of divine revelation, including the early work composed prior to his declaration of mission (mostly those written in Baghdad, but also a few that have survived from his time in Tehran and Kurdistán). All told, there are at least 15,000 'Tablets' by him, mostly letters, but also including a number of substantial works.

Bahá'u'lláh's early writings have already been mentioned. The themes of this period were continued in his later work, specifically his awareness of the divine presence; ethics and the spiritual path; the divine summons; and the nature of God's relationship with humankind and creation. Later writings include his addresses to world rulers, and subjects such as the proper form of government and international order, and the establishment of Bahá'í law. In contrast to Bábism, there is relatively little concern for esotericism.

Bahá'u'lláh's Awareness of the Divine Presence

Throughout his ministry, Bahá'u'lláh emphasized the magnitude of his sense of the divine presence. Although he gave this theological form in the doctrine that the Manifestation of God expresses the attributes of God to humanity (God in essence being utterly transcendent and removed from the possibility of human contact), the force of much of Bahá'u'lláh's writings here defies easy description, giving as it does an impression of both the ineffability and immediacy of the relationship he felt with the Godhead.

Several of his writings take the form of dialogues between the voices of God and Bahá'u'lláh, such as the 'Fire Tablet' in which Bahá'u'lláh bewails his sufferings in the path of God and God comforts him. Another recurrent form is the description of a vision of a heavenly messenger or the personification of a divine attribute, such as Trustworthiness in all her beauty, 'standing on a pillar of light' (Bahá'u'lláh, *Tablets* 122). At times speaking directly with the voice of God, Bahá'u'lláh elsewhere compares himself to a leaf stirred by the winds of God's will, and transformed by him – wishing to be silent, but aroused by the Holy Spirit and bidden to speak (Shoghi Effendi, *God Passes By* 102).

Ethics and the Spiritual Path

From the Baghdad period onwards, Bahá'u'lláh emphasized the spiritual and ethical requirements of the 'true seeker' after God. Although at times employing the phraseology of Sufism and referring to mystical states of soul that transcend everyday experience, he was far more concerned with outlining the ethical and religious requirements of daily life. Central here are such traditional Islamic concerns as the need for detachment from the world, devotional prayer, and the fear of and trust in God, but there is also a distinctive stress on practical activity. Particular qualities emphasized include the need for complete trustworthiness and honesty in all social dealings; wisdom; righteousness; charity; kindness to all, including animals; forgiveness; steadfastness; patience; humility and avoidance of backbiting.

The Divine Summons

This is 'the day of God', in which the whole human race is called upon to recognize God's messenger. In the *Íqán*, the messenger was still the Báb, but after his declaration of mission it was Bahá'u'lláh. Bahá'u'lláh is the promised one of the religions of the past, and in various of his writings he addresses the Zoroastrians, the Jews, and particularly the Christians, in addition to the followers of Islam. The religious leaders are specifically summoned, historically having been responsible for the persecution and opposition to each of the previous Manifestations of God.

The Islamic (and Bábí) teaching of holy war is abolished; the Bahá'ís are to teach the Faith through their words and deeds. If necessary, they are to welcome martyrdom, but living to establish their cause in the world is the goal. Those who persecute the faithful are condemned, and Bahá'u'lláh states that they will be chastised by God. The Shí'í 'ulamá of Iran are particularly warned of their eventual abasement if they persist in their opposition.

Theology and Metaphysics

Bahá'u'lláh's theology revolves around the Manifestations of God. God is in essence unknowable and can only be approached through his attributes, and these are most perfectly expressed in the persons of the Manifestations of God. The Manifestations combine divine and human qualities. Each one brings a renewal of God's grace and gives his followers the teachings appropriate for that particular age, and on that basis a new divine civilization develops. In addition to the prophets listed in the Qur'án (notably Adam, Abraham, Moses, Jesus and Muhammad), Bahá'u'lláh recognizes Zoroaster as a Manifestation – and 'Abdu'l-

Bahá was later to recognize Krishna and the Buddha. The purpose of human life is to recognize God through the current Manifestation and to love him and obey his laws. Such action leads the believer to 'heaven' in both this life and the afterlife, while opposition leads to 'hell'. Heaven and hell are thus regarded as spiritual states: there is no bodily resurrection; and creation is eternal.

The Addresses to the Rulers

Bahá'u'lláh's proclamation to the rulers consisted of a number of letters sent to specific individuals (Sultán Abdulazíz, Násiri'd-Dín Sháh, Napoleon III, Queen Victoria, Czar Alexander II and Pope Pius IX), and to ministers in the Ottoman government. Notional addresses to particular kings and to political and religious leaders in general can also be found in various of his writings, such as the *Súriy-i-Mulúk* (*Chapter of the Kings*, 1868) and the *Kitáb-i-Aqdas* (*The Most Holy Book*, c.1873). Three main elements may be identified in these writings: the announcement of Bahá'u'lláh's claims, reproof or praise addressed to particular rulers, and comments on the nature of government and international order. The first two represent an extension of his proclamation of the divine summons, the third will be dealt with separately below.

Bahá'u'lláh declares himself to be the king of kings. The kings are his vassals, but he has not come to seize their kingdoms. They are bidden to turn towards God and investigate his cause. It is nearness to God, not sovereignty, that is the source of glory. In his letters to the Western monarchs he also states that he is the fulfilment of Christian prophecy and the return of Christ.

Of the addresses to individual rulers, the letters to

Násiri'd-Dín Sháh and to Sultán Abdulazíz and his ministers had an immediate importance in that between them, the two rulers controlled the fate of Bahá'u'lláh and that of the majority of the Bahá'ís. The letter to the Sultan (1863) appears to have been strongly worded and challenging, and this could certainly be said of subsequent letters to his leading ministers and a nominal address to him in the *Súriy-i-Mulúk*. The actions of the Ottoman government in unjustly subjecting Bahá'u'lláh and his companions to successive exiles without making proper enquiry are condemned; the Sultan is counselled not to abandon the affairs of state into the hands of untrustworthy and impious ministers; and predictions are made that the Sultan will fall from the 'throne of tyranny' and that European Turkey will be lost. Abdulazíz's later deposition (1876) and the disastrous Ottoman defeat by the Russians in 1877–8, which included the occupation of Edirne and led to the loss of Eastern Roumelia, did much to enhance Bahá'u'lláh's prestige in Iran, leading to at least one prominent conversion.

By contrast, the letter to the Shah (delivered in 1868) is conciliatory in tone, emphasizing the loyalty and peaceableness of the Bahá'ís, now transformed under Bahá'u'lláh's guidance from the militant Bábís of old, and asking that they should be given official recognition and protection. That this appeal was unsuccessful cannot have been surprising, and elsewhere in his writings Bahá'u'lláh condemns Násiri'd-Dín Sháh as the 'Prince of Oppressors', consoling the Bahá'ís with the promise that Tehran would one day be blessed with a just ruler who would protect them.

The letters to the Western rulers had more symbolic value, indicating the universality of Bahá'u'lláh's proclamation. Some sort of request for French assistance in securing justice for the Bahá'ís in the Ottoman Empire was apparently made; the manner of Napoleon III's rejection of this was deemed arrogant, and the prediction was made in a second letter – copies of which were widely circulated – that he would be deposed and France thrown into confusion. France's subsequent defeat in the Franco-Prussian War (1870–1) again enhanced Bahá'u'lláh's prestige among the Iranian Bahá'ís.

Of the other Western rulers to whom letters were sent, two were praised: Alexander II for the assistance afforded to Bahá'u'lláh by the Russian ambassador in Tehran at the time of his imprisonment, and Queen Victoria for the British system of parliamentary (rather than absolutist) government – the letter was written the year after the 1867 Reform Act – and for the abolition of the slave trade. The Pope was instructed to abandon his temporal domains (the Papal States) and to expend the Church's wealth in the path of God. All three were summoned to accept Bahá'u'lláh. Of those addressed in the *Aqdas* (but to whom no letters were actually sent), the Austro-Hungarian Emperor Franz Joseph was rebuked for his heedlessness in failing to enquire about Bahá'u'lláh when he visited Jerusalem. The rulers and presidents of the Americas were bidden to crush injustice. The German Kaiser Wilhelm I was reminded of the transience of conquest and of the former glory of his defeated adversary, Napoleon III – the prophecy was also made that the banks of the Rhine would be 'covered with gore' as a result of retribution, that Germany would have 'another turn' and that Berlin would lament. However one chooses to interpret Bahá'u'lláh's prescience, these several predictions are well authenticated, and again attracted much attention in Iran at the end of World War I.

Government and World Order

A component part of his letters to the rulers, but also a recurring theme in many of Bahá'u'lláh's letters of the 'Akká period, was his prescription for the remodelling of government and international order. These topics also received considerable attention in 'Abdu'l-Bahá's treatise on Iranian 'modernization' (*The Secret of Divine Civilization*, 1875), which was anonymously circulated within Iranian intellectual circles at this time, and came to form part of the Bahá'í textual tradition.

On the subject of government, Bahá'u'lláh and 'Abdu'l-Bahá are adamant as to the necessity for just rule. If rulers do not protect their subjects from oppression, they will be answerable before God. It is God who has given them dominion and this brings with it a heavy responsibility, particularly to guard the poor and defenceless. It is by their people's means that they subsist, and they must therefore ensure that the people are guarded from both political and economic injustice (the latter evidenced in the gross inequalities found in a city such as Istanbul). They must rule in accordance with divine commandments. Attachment to wealth will not profit them, for they will eventually be brought to their tombs. In obvious contrast to Lockean liberalism, no justification is given for rebellion against an unjust king, however. The system of constitutional monarchy (with its combination of kingship – regarded as a sign of God – and democracy) is praised; rulers are counselled to appoint officials on the basis of merit and to ensure that they do not become despotic; importance is placed on having an educated electorate, to lessen the likelihood of political corruption; and the vital role played by religion in the preservation of social stability is emphasized.

Internationally, the rulers should seek reconciliation and amity, so that they may reduce their armaments and the burden of taxation on their people. The rights of each nation should be guaranteed by the practice of collective security, whereby all nations undertake to unite in opposition to any aggressor. A world tribunal would act as arbitrator when conflicts emerged. The governments should also select a single language and script to be taught throughout the world as auxiliaries to the various mother tongues.

Beyond this limited peace between nations, Bahá'u'lláh also summoned the peoples of the world to what he termed the 'Most Great Peace', the unification of religions and races and the transformation of the world into a single homeland in which the people would be as the 'leaves of one tree'.

For the Bahá'ís, strict obedience and loyalty to established governments is enjoined, and they are forbidden to meddle in politics. They are, however, to work for the betterment of the world and to promote education, agriculture and the arts, crafts and sciences.

Bahá'u'lláh's attitude to the West was nuanced. Unlike the Iran of the Bábís in the 1840s, the Ottoman Empire in the 1860s was already subject to a considerable Western influence, and the ideas of modernization on Western lines were much discussed by the Ottoman reformers with whom Bahá'u'lláh (and 'Abdu'l-Bahá) were in contact (see Cole). The stance of the Bahá'í prophet and his son was to advocate the adoption of Western-style constitutionalism and elected assemblies, along with the wholesale adoption of Western technology and organizational techniques, as had occurred in Japan. By themselves such reforms were regarded as insufficient, however. What was at least equally needed was a religious, moral and educational reformation. Also of major significance was their critique of Western materialism; they considered that Western civilization had become unbalanced through its loss of contact with God.

Holy Law

Like the Báb, Bahá'u'lláh composed a book of holy law, the *Kitáb-i-Aqdas*, or *Most Holy Book*. This was completed in about 1873 whilst he was still in the city of 'Akká. It was supplemented by

Bahá'u'lláh's replies to questions raised about it, and by other of his writings. Significantly, it was written partly in response to requests by Bahá'ís for a book of laws.

The *Aqdas* lays down a double obligation on all human beings: recognition of Bahá'u'lláh and obedience to his laws. These laws are from God and constitute both the best means for the maintenance of social and world order and a spiritual wine for those who love God. The detailed laws include the following obligations: individual daily ritual prayer, remembrance of God and recitation of scripture; an annual nineteen-day fast; payment of a religious tax, the 'right of God' (*ḥuqúqu'lláh*), to the centre of the Faith; that Bahá'ís follow a trade or profession – such work counting as a form of worship – and avoid idleness; that fathers instruct their sons and daughters to read and write and ensure that they receive both a religious and academic education; service to the Bahá'í Cause; and the writing of a will. Bahá'ís are also enjoined to observe great cleanliness, delicacy and propriety in their conduct and to follow a moral life. In contrast to Islam, these obligations are made matters of conscience, and only in the case of the duty to ensure that a child learns to read is communal regulation involved.

Prohibitions include backbiting, calumny, contention and conflict, the kissing of hands (as of a religious leader to show deference), seeking absolution for sins from another person, shaving one's head, trading in slaves, begging, sedition, gambling, the use of intoxicants (including alcohol, opium and hashish) and asceticism. Murder, theft, arson and adultery are also forbidden and appropriate punishments specified.

Various Islamic and Bábí laws and practices are abrogated, including Islamic restrictions on music (described by Bahá'u'lláh as a ladder for the soul) and the use of gold and silver utensils; the Islamic (particularly Shí'í) concept of ritual purity; and the

Bayanic laws regarding the destruction of non-Bábí books and the prohibition of marriage with non-believers. In marked contrast to all forms of religious exclusivism, the Bahá'ís are bidden to associate with the followers of all religions in friendship and peace.

Other ordinances in the *Aqdas* include marriage (recommended but not obligatory, forbidden to those under the age of fifteen – the age of maturity – and dependent on the consent of the bride, the groom and their parents); the limitation of polygamy to two wives at most (one being regarded as preferable and 'Abdu'l-Bahá later abolishing polygamy altogether); the condemnation of divorce (which is nevertheless permitted subject to a year of waiting); a detailed system for inheritance in the case of intestacy; the form of burial; and the institution of the 'House of Justice' as a Bahá'í administrative body to be established in every city, and of the Bahá'í House of Worship as a place for prayer.

'Abdu'l-Bahá

Bahá'u'lláh named 'Abdu'l-Bahá the 'Master' (*Áqá*) and the 'Most Great Branch' (*Ghuṣn-i-A'zam*), and in his will appointed him to be the head of his religion after him. 'Abbás himself chose be known by the title 'Abdu'l-Bahá ('Servant of Bahá').

Born in 1844 – according to tradition on the very night of the Báb's declaration – 'Abbás Effendi ('Abdu'l-Bahá) was his father's eldest surviving son. His mother was Ásíyih Khánum (d. 1886), the first of Bahá'u'lláh's three wives. Of his immediate siblings, only his sister, Bahiyyih (1846–1932), outlived their father, becoming one of 'Abdu'l-Bahá's most important aides. He had in addition three half-brothers and two half-sisters by Bahá'u'lláh's other wives. During the period of the Baghdad exile, when he was in his teens, he began to assist his father, and in Edirne and 'Akká took responsibility for the practical management of the large household of Bahá'u'lláh's family and disciples. He also acted as one of his father's secretaries. Although never attending any school, he evidently read widely and became well known and respected amongst Ottoman officials and reformers, including several of the provincial governors in their various places of exile. After his father moved out of 'Akká in 1877, 'Abdu'l-Bahá continued to live in the city, increasingly gaining acceptance as a local notable despite living under the government's order of banishment. Giving alms to the poor and regularly attending the local mosque, he was regarded as a pious, albeit heterodox

'Abdu'l-Bahá

Muslim leader rather than as the son of the founder of a new religion. He married Munírih Nahrí (1847–1938), a member of a prominent Isfahán Bahá'í merchant family, in 1873. The couple had four daughters who survived to adulthood, in addition to two sons and three daughters who died in childhood. Unlike his father, grandfather and uncles, all of whom followed the contemporary upper-class Muslim practice of having several wives, 'Abdu'l-Bahá remained monogamous, later interpreting the Bahá'í marriage law so as to prohibit polygamy.

Most of 'Abdu'l-Bahá's writings and recorded oral teachings date from after 1892, but already during his father's lifetime he had written a treatise on what we would now term the 'modernization' of Iran (*The Secret of Divine Civilization*, 1875, see above), as well as a short history of the Bábí and Bahá'í religions (*A Traveller's Narrative*, 1886, originally published under the translator's name, Edward G. Browne).

Succession and Ministry

The period of 'Abdu'l-Bahá's leadership of the Bahá'ís (1892–1921) witnessed a number of important developments in the Faith, including the growth of the first Bahá'í communities in the West and significant changes in those of Iran and Turkistan. These will be discussed below (see chapter 8), but we should note here how crucial was 'Abdu'l-Bahá's guidance and co-ordination. His contact with the Bahá'ís was mostly through a vast interchange of correspondence, which continued throughout his ministry. He also received large numbers of Bahá'í pilgrims and met with Bahá'ís during his visits to Egypt and the West (1911–13).

'Abdu'l-Bahá's own ministry can be divided into three phases. The first phase began in 1892, when he assumed the leadership of the Faith as 'the centre of Bahá'u'lláh's covenant' and the interpreter of his writings. Most of the Bahá'ís readily accepted this appointment and gave him their devotion. Many members of Bahá'u'lláh's extended family, however, led by 'Abdu'l-Bahá's half-brother Muhammad-'Alí, were unwilling to accept his authority. A covert and later open campaign to discredit him followed. Only 'Abdu'l-Bahá's sister, wife and daughters, together with a surviving uncle and his family, remained loyal. The followers of 'Abdu'l-Bahá plausibly accused Muhammad-'Alí of being motivated by intense jealousy. For their part, the followers of Muhammad-'Alí accused 'Abdu'l-Bahá of overreaching the mandate given to him by his father.

Although it was unable to shake the allegiance of the mass of the Bahá'ís, this campaign was to lead to recurrent problems for 'Abdu'l-Bahá with the Turkish authorities, including the reimposition of confinement in 'Akká (1901) and the threat of exile to North Africa. This prolonged opposition caused 'Abdu'l-Bahá to give great emphasis to the doctrine that there was a sacred Covenant that ensured the preservation of Bahá'í unity through obedience to the properly appointed leaders of the Faith. Those who broke this Covenant, such as Muhammad-'Alí and his associates, were denounced as 'Covenant-breakers' and were ultimately excommunicated.

It was also during these years that he began to encourage the formation of locally elected Bahá'í councils in the various parts of the Bahá'í world, as well as of several 'national' bodies. Again, he wrote his *Will and Testament*, in which he appointed his eldest grandson, Shoghi Effendi – then still a child – to be the Guardian of the Faith after him; outlined the system to be employed for the election of the Universal House of Justice referred to by Bahá'u'lláh; and exposed the attacks directed against him by his half-brothers, excluding Muhammad-'Alí from succession because of his Covenant-breaking. The provisions of

The shrine of the Báb on Mount Carmel
Top: The original limestone building commissioned by 'Abdu'l-Bahá
Bottom. After the completion of the superstructure in 1953

the will remained secret until after 'Abdu'l-Bahá's death in 1921, but it is clear that he wished to ensure that the Faith would remain co-ordinated and protected from his opponents even if something were to happen to him.

These years also saw the composition of his *Treatise on Politics* (1892–3), written for the Iranian Bahá'ís to guide them through the politically troubled period then beginning; the first pilgrimage visit from Western Bahá'ís (1898–9); 'Abdu'l-Bahá's encouragement of educational, medical and economic development among the Eastern Bahá'ís; and the beginning of the construction of the first Bahá'í House of Worship in the city of Ashkhabad in Russian Turkistan.

The second phase of 'Abdu'l-Bahá's ministry began in 1908, when the dangers that had faced him in 'Akká ended following the Young Turk revolution of that year and the freeing of Ottoman political prisoners. Soon afterwards he moved across the bay from 'Akká to the newly developing city of Haifa, which henceforth was to remain the headquarters of the Faith. Haifa's spiritual significance for Bahá'ís was established by the burial there in 1909 of the remains of the Báb, which had been smuggled out of Iran some years previously. The main part of what is now the inner shrine of the Báb was completed under 'Abdu'l-Bahá's direction at a site selected by Bahá'u'lláh on the slopes of Mount Carmel.

Taking advantage of his new freedom of movement, 'Abdu'l-Bahá, now in his late sixties and in poor health, travelled to Egypt in 1910, and then determined to visit the new Bahá'ís of the West, embarking on the first of his Western journeys (to London, Bristol and Paris) in 1911. Resting for the winter in Egypt, he made a longer second journey from March 1912 to June 1913, and during fourteen months of extensive travelling visited thirty-eight American and Canadian cities before proceeding

'Abdu'l-Bahá in Woking, England, 1913

'Abdu'l-Bahá in Paris

'Abdu'l-Bahá in Mr Milburn's church, Chicago, 1912

'Abdu'l-Bahá in Stuttgart, 1913

to Europe, where he visited Britain, France, Germany and Austria–Hungary. His public addresses during these journeys represent an important addition to Bahá'í scripture.

The journeys themselves contributed to the consolidation of the fledgling Western Bahá'í communities, giving the Bahá'ís a wider vision of their Faith and encouraging them to greater action. They also attracted considerable sympathetic newspaper attention, and 'Abdu'l-Bahá met many eminent people, including churchmen such as Archdeacon Wilberforce and T. K. Cheyne in England; academics such as the comparative religionist J. Estlin Carpenter, David Starr Jordan of Stanford University, the orientalist Arminius Vambéry, and the philosophers John Dewey and Henri Bergson; the suffragette leader Emmeline Pankhurst; Annie Besant, the president of the Theosophical Society; and the author Kahlil Gibran.

Given his status as an Iranian exile and former Ottoman prisoner, his reception in the United States by the Turkish ambassador and the Iranian chargé d'affaires (at that time a Bahá'í) were particularly significant. Apart from meeting dignitaries and members of sympathetic organizations such as peace societies and the Esperantists, 'Abdu'l-Bahá on several occasions made a point of visiting the poor, and in Washington DC, he very deliberately scandalized social convention by insisting that a leading black Bahá'í should sit next to him at a prestigious dinner. His weary conclusion that a European war was imminent also attracted attention.

With 'Abdu'l-Bahá's return to Egypt (June 1913) and later to Haifa (December), the third and final phase of his ministry began. At first exhausted by his journeys, he was soon effectively confined to Palestine by the onset of World War I (1914–18). During that conflict, 'Abdu'l-Bahá's life was again threatened – by the Turkish army chief, Jamál Páshá – but this danger ended with the collapse of Turkish rule. The war years and their immediate aftermath also brought famine to Palestine, and 'Abdu'l-Bahá averted local catastrophe by supplying grain stocks. He gained the respect of the newly established British authorities, who secured him the award of a knighthood in 1920.

The final three years of 'Abdu'l-Bahá's life were spent peace-fully attending to the work of directing the affairs of the Faith. In addition to being a prominent and widely respected local notable, he was now clearly recognized as the head of an inter-national religious movement. In addition to his contacts with Bahá'ís, he was in contact with the executive committee of the Central Organization for a Durable Peace, based at The Hague, to whom he indicated that the League of Nations, then about to come into being, was not to be equated with Bahá'u'lláh's supreme tribunal, being insufficient to establish universal peace. Elsewhere, he also warned of the limitations of the Paris peace

'Abdu'l-Bahá's investiture, Haifa, 1920

settlement: the vanquished powers would rekindle the flames of conflict, he said, and the Balkans would remain an area of chronic instability. He predicted that 'the Movement of the Left' and other movements that would emerge would gain great influence ('Abdu'l-Bahá, *Selections* 249–50, 306).

'Abdu'l-Bahá died on 28 November 1921, his funeral being marked by the great number and religious diversity of its mourners. He was buried in a separate part of the Báb's shrine. He was survived by his sister, wife and daughters and their families.

Any consideration of 'Abdu'l-Bahá's leadership must include some reference to his character. Many non-Bahá'ís referred to him as a powerful personality, and he evidently greatly impressed E. G. Browne, who wrote of his eloquence, wide religious knowledge, and 'majestic' and 'genial' bearing (*Traveller's Narrative* vol. II, xxxvi). He was both a commanding presence and intensely approachable, with a ready sense of humour. The accounts left

The funeral procession of 'Abdu'l-Bahá, 29 November 1921

by many Bahá'ís, of course, are particularly laudatory, emphasizing the enormous devotion they felt towards him. Many Western Bahá'ís were inclined to see him in Christ-like terms as the personification of love and compassion.

Writings and Talks

Since 'Abdu'l-Bahá was regarded as the authoritative interpreter of his father's works, his own writings and authenticated talks formed a major addition to the Bahá'í 'canon': over 27,000 of his letters have survived. There is also a substantial body of unauthenticated 'pilgrim's notes' of conversations with him. His writings prior to his succession as leader – notably *The Secret of Divine Civilization* – were readily accorded the same status as his later writings.

'Abdu'l-Bahá's Western writings and talks are of particular significance. His letters to Western Bahá'ís, recorded conversations with visiting Bahá'í pilgrims, and addresses to Bahá'ís and the general public during his tours of Europe and North America, all reflect his responses to Western concerns and indicate the manner in which he thought it appropriate to present the Faith to Westerners. A wide range of topics was dealt with, including discourses on various Christian subjects, and Western social issues such as the emancipation of women and industrial relations. 'Abdu'l-Bahá's responses demonstrate an extensive knowledge and understanding of what to him was an alien world. Although always making use of interpreters (mostly Iranians, but also including some Western Bahá'ís who had learned Persian), it appears that 'Abdu'l-Bahá had some knowledge of English in addition to his native Persian, Turkish and Arabic.

In his public talks in the West, 'Abdu'l-Bahá frequently presented a list of Bahá'í principles (ranging from nine to fourteen, the number varied), this listing of principles henceforth becoming a common element in Bahá'í literature. The principles listed included the following:

• Each individual should independently investigate truth, putting aside historical prejudices. Thus will they find the one reality that is common to all.

• All divine religions are one; they are expressions of a single reality. The teachings of Bahá'u'lláh best represent the 'universal religion' needed at the present time.

• Genuine religion is a powerful support for social stability: without it crime and irreligion flourish.

• For all its fruits, material civilization by itself is not sufficient to promote human progress. Only when combined with 'divine civilization' and empowered by the Holy Spirit will it be the cause of genuine advance.

• Religion should be the cause of love and unity. If a particular religion only produces hatred and division then it is no longer an expression of true religion and should be abandoned.

• Religion must be in conformity with science and reason; if it is not, then it is only ignorant superstition.

• Bahá'u'lláh has come to establish the Most Great Peace. An international tribunal should now be instituted to adjudicate disputes between nations.

• The whole human race is one, all human beings are equally the children of God, the only differences between them being those of education and spiritual health.

• Religious, racial, political, national and class prejudices are destructive and based on ignorance; they cause strife and impede moral progress.

• Human progress cannot occur as long as people are still forced to struggle for their daily existence.

• Extremes of wealth and more especially of poverty are to be abolished, and all are to have access to the necessities of life.
• All individuals are to be equal before the law, and justice is to be securely established in society.
• Women are the equals of men and are to have equality of rights, particularly of educational opportunity. Without such equality the progress of both sexes is impeded.
• All children are to receive an education.
• There should be an international auxiliary language.

Although derived in large part from the principles delineated by Bahá'u'lláh, these lists and the talks in which particular principles were described in more detail show significant differences in emphasis. This is most obvious in the advocacy of the emancipation and equality of women, a principle that appears to have received little more than passing reference from Bahá'u'lláh, but which was discussed at length by 'Abdu'l-Bahá. Again, 'Abdu'l-Bahá dealt with economic questions, education, the critique of materialistic philosophies, and the principle of racial equality in far more detail than his father had.

One work that later came to have great significance was a series of letters addressed to the North American Bahá'ís during World War I. These *Tablets of the Divine Plan* (1916–17) call on the Bahá'ís to undertake a campaign of teaching to establish the Bahá'í Faith throughout not only all the American states and Canadian provinces, but in all parts of the world.

Bahá'í Communities, 1866–1921

Bahá'u'lláh clearly conceived of his religion as a universal creed, destined to spread in the course of time to the whole world. Therefore, a major theme in the writings of both Bahá'u'lláh and 'Abdu'l-Bahá was the need to 'teach the Cause', and expand both the numbers of believers and the religion's geographical spread. From the outset, the movement was imbued with a strong missionary ethos, and a widespread expansion was soon set in train. This expansion was concentrated in Iran, but also came to include the Caucasus (1860s), Egypt (1860s), India and Burma (1870s), Russian Turkistan (1880s), and North America and Europe (1890s). The idea of worldwide expansion was given special emphasis in 'Abdu'l-Bahá's *Tablets of the Divine Plan*. The establishment of Bahá'í communities in the West bore a particular significance as a major 'cultural breakthrough', indicating the potential universality of the Bahá'í Cause.

Iran

Bahá'í expansion in Iran initially built on the existing network of Bábí groups, which had already been partly reanimated through the efforts of Bahá'u'lláh. Although in some towns there was a division into rival factions and even violence between Bahá'í and Azalí partisans, the majority of the Bábí community became Bahá'ís within a few years of Bahá'u'lláh's first dispatch of missionary emissaries in 1866. Responding to a forceful charismatic leadership, the Bábís – now Bahá'ís – displayed a ready zeal and resourcefulness in the consolidation and expansion of their community. They were effectively reborn as a religious force within Iranian society, a fact quickly recognized by both the state and Muslim authorities and by resident and visiting foreigners.

We do not know the extent of the Bahá'í expansion that followed. It is possible that by the 1880s, their numbers were again in the region of 100,000 – the same figure often given for the number of Bábís before the movement had been crushed – and that thirty years later, the number was almost certainly in excess of this (Smith, 'Numbers'). More definitely, it is clear that contemporaries recognized the religion's dynamism at this time, and that a significant number of converts was made. These new Bahá'ís included men of considerable prominence such as clerics, government officials and even members of the Qájár family. From the 1880s, they also included substantial numbers of the Jewish and Zoroastrian minorities (though not of the Armenian and Assyrian Christian population). Most significantly of all, the movement now appears to have undergone a process of 'familialization', with the conversion and much fuller involvement of wives and daughters, and hence the assurance of effective socialization of Bahá'í children and the continuance of the movement over time. There was also a wider circle of sympathizers and secret Bahá'ís, including, according to one account, Mírzá Shírází, the leading Shí'í divine of the age (Balyuzi, *Eminent Bahá'ís* 252–60).

Internal consolidation of the movement became increasingly effective, with the various local Bahá'í communities being linked together by visits from leading Bahá'ís and the receipt of regular correspondence from Bahá'u'lláh delivered by itinerant Bahá'í couriers. Prominent individual Bahá'ís were often given specific missions by Bahá'u'lláh. In 1887–8, four were appointed 'Hands of the Cause', and in time they played a key organizing role in what was increasingly a unified national Bahá'í community. Although many of the Bahá'í leaders at this time still came from clerical backgrounds (including some of the new converts), non-clerics attained far more prominence than had been the case in the Bábí community.

The rising level of Bahá'í activity could only provoke opposition from the 'ulamá. Some local governors and clerics were protective of the Bahá'ís, but in many areas persecution became commonplace, with a number of instances of beatings and imprisonment, and even murder – often by mobs stirred up by clerical sermons – or execution. Of the executions, three were particularly noteworthy: of Badí', the youth who delivered Bahá'u'lláh's letter to Násiri'd-Dín Sháh in 1869; and of two brothers who were leading Isfahání merchants in 1879. The execution of the merchants indicated that no Bahá'í was safe, no matter how socially prominent. The brothers' execution is also significant in that, as was widely recognized at the time, religious motives were deliberately used to mask financial greed on the part of one of the leading local clerics (who was in debt to the brothers) and the compliant governor. Henceforth, persecution often assumed a financial as well as religious *raison d'être*, disguising either extortion or theft. As declared apostates, according to Shí'í sacred law the Bahá'ís could be killed with impunity and their goods seized by pious Muslims.

For their part, the Bahá'ís responded peacefully. As Bahá'u'lláh insisted, the days of Bábí militancy were past. The often heroic fortitude of the Bahá'ís in these circumstances served to attract further converts, as well as the sympathetic attention of foreign diplomats and of some members of the governing élite. Wider knowledge of Bahá'í – as opposed to Bábí –

beliefs spread through society.

The situation changed under 'Abdu'l-Bahá's leadership, in part because of increasing political and social unrest, which finally led to the collapse of the Qájár regime and the military intervention of the Russians and British. In this troubled period, it was extremely difficult to steer a stable course. 'Abdu'l-Bahá continued Bahá'u'lláh's policy of emphasizing loyalty to the government, and under a new Shah (Muzaffari'd-Dín, who reigned from 1896 to 1907) there seemed to be real possibilities of securing protection for the community. Many Bahá'ís occupied important government positions at this time, including several provincial governorships. Unfortunately for the Bahá'ís, the Qájár regime itself was now increasingly ineffective, and the Bahá'ís became an easy target for displaced political discontent, several pogroms being organized against them.

In the face of these difficulties, the Bahá'ís seem to have become more rather than less confident of the success of their mission. The increasing turmoil perhaps gave them a sense of the possibilities for the transformation of society and a sudden victory. If so, this was augmented by news of the successes of the Faith in Turkistan and America, as well as by the arrival of a small number of American Bahá'ís to help with the establishment of Bahá'í schools and a clinic. The progress of 'the Cause' in the world was becoming palpable.

This was also a period of administrative development within the Bahá'í community. On 'Abdu'l-Bahá's instruction, the Hands of the Cause in Tehran formed a consulting assembly in 1897 to advise and direct the Bahá'ís. This soon became a partly elected body, and a variety of committees were formed to manage activities ranging from child education to poor relief, publishing and the adjudication of commercial disputes between Bahá'ís. Assemblies were also formed in other major Bahá'í centres, the Tehran assembly assuming the role of a central directorate. One important aspect of these developments was concern for the advancement of women, a separate assembly for Bahá'í women being established in 1910. A Bahá'í benevolent fund was also formed.

The Ottoman Empire and Egypt

From the 1860s onwards, small Bahá'í groups were established in various parts of the Ottoman Empire and Egypt. Initially, these consisted almost entirely of Iranian expatriates. The potential vulnerability of these Bahá'ís was vividly illustrated during the 1860s by the arrest of Bahá'ís in Egypt and Baghdad and their exile to the Sudan and Mosul respectively. A small number of Levantine Christians and Sunnís were converted, but in general missionary work was avoided in these areas, perhaps out of sensitivity for the effects this might have on the authorities' dealings with the Bahá'í colony in 'Akká.

This policy changed in Egypt in the 1890s, when the distinguished Bahá'í scholar Mírzá Abu'l-Fadl (1844–1914) established himself at al-Azhar University, the leading seat of learning in the Muslim world. A number of conversions followed and a small but dedicated community of indigenous Egyptian Bahá'ís came into being.

India and Burma

Several Indian Muslims converted to Bábism in Iran, but it was not until the Bahá'í period that a community of believers was established in what was then British India. A key figure here was the Bahá'í teacher Sulaymán Khán Tunakábuní, who travelled widely in the sub-continent during the 1870s. A small network of Bahá'ís came into being in several cities, mostly in northern India. They were largely from the Persian-educated minority. With the newly converted Sayyid Muṣṭáfá Rúmí, Sulaymán Khán then moved to South-East Asia, where a Bahá'í community was established amongst the Muslims of Burma.

Further progress in India occurred during 'Abdu'l-Bahá's ministry, with the conversion of a number of both immigrant Iranian Zoroastrians and native Parsees in Bombay and of a small circle of highly educated Indians in other cities, including a high-caste Hindu and a Sikh, both of whom became prominent in work for the further expansion of the Faith. There were some moves towards administrative development, including the formation of a national teaching council (1911), and publishing work was undertaken, but the Indian Bahá'ís remained strongly 'élitist' in their approach, with much emphasis being placed on public lectures. Their numbers remained small.

Russian Turkistan and Caucasia

Of greater immediate significance was the development of Bahá'í communities in the Russian territories bordering Iran. The first of these was Russian Azerbaiján, where existing Bábí groups were converted from the 1860s onwards. There was subsequent expansion to other parts of the Caucasus. In Turkistan the most important of the Bahá'í communities was at Ashkhabad, the capital of the newly established province of Transcaspia (1881). Bahá'ís were among the immigrants from Iran to the new city, and by 1889 they numbered about 400, including many builders and merchants. Intent on importing the pattern of Iranian persecutions, immigrant Shí'í activists then plotted a general attack on the Ashkhabad Bahá'ís. In the event, only one man was murdered, and to the astonishment of the Shí'ís, the murderers were arrested by the Russian authorities and later tried. An initial sentence of death was later commuted to one of life imprisonment following intercession by the Bahá'ís. This was a major turning point for the Bahá'ís: for the first time in their history, their persecutors had been apprehended and punished. The Russian territories were henceforth to be seen as an attractive refuge as well as an area of economic opportunity, and Bahá'í immigration surged. By 1917, the Bahá'í community comprised about 4,000 people.

Freed from their former constraints, the Bahá'ís openly established a wide range of Bahá'í institutions, including a public bath, a travellers' hospice, a dispensary and hospital, schools and a printing press. Of greatest public note was an imposing Bahá'í Temple, which was substantially completed by 1907. This structure was the first Bahá'í House of Worship in the world.

A group of prominent Bahá'í merchants and former clerics initially provided the Ashkhabad community with leadership, but in 1895–6 they were replaced by an elected council, also possibly the first in the world. This in turn appointed committees to oversee the various aspects of Bahá'í community life. Bahá'í groups were also established in several other parts of the Russian Empire, including Samarkand and Moscow, but the number of Bahá'ís in these places remained small. There were a few Russian converts, but generally there was no attempt to convert ethnic Russians, as this would have been illegal.

Following the Russian Revolution of 1917, there was a great increase in Bahá'í activity in the Russian territories, including the conversion of a number of ethnic Russians. This period came to an end in the mid-1920s as the new Soviet regime established its authority and implemented policies against organized religions.

The West

The establishment of Bahá'í communities in the West marked a major and decisive transition in Bahá'í history. Hitherto, despite the conversion of a small number of non-Muslims in the Middle East, the Bahá'í Faith had essentially remained a phenomenon within Islam: Iranian Jews and Zoroastrians and Levantine Christians still operated within an Islamic cultural environment and shared many of its values. With the conversion of Bahá'ís in the West, the Faith entered a new cultural milieu. Although in total numbers the Western Bahá'ís were relatively few, their inclusion in the Faith had far-reaching consequences. For the first time, the Bahá'í Faith became a genuinely international movement, and its cultural adaptability was vividly demonstrated. Moreover, despite their small numbers, the Western Bahá'ís enjoyed a freedom and access to resources that enabled them to play a vital role in the further expansion of the Faith.

The initial breakthrough occurred in the United States, where a small Bahá'í group was established in Chicago in 1894. The Chicago group then expanded rapidly, while a large number of smaller groups soon developed elsewhere in the USA, and also in Canada and in Paris and London, so that by 1900 there were probably well over 1,500 Western Bahá'ís.

This initial growth centred on the activities of one Bahá'í teacher, Ibrahim George Kheiralla (1849–1929), himself a recent convert of Syrian Christian background, who was able to express the Bahá'í teachings in a way that appealed to Western Christians. Thereafter, further expansion reflected the geographical mobility of American society.

As it first developed, the fledgling American community was somewhat heterodox in Bahá'í terms. Kheiralla's interpretation of the Bahá'í Faith was idiosyncratic and many of the early

Bahá'ís were drawn from the cultic fringe of small groups of religious seekers then beginning to flourish. Relating the Bahá'í Faith to an esoteric version of the Christian Adventist tradition, Kheiralla also distanced it from its Islamic roots. These misconceptions were gradually eradicated from 1900 onwards with the arrival of a series of more knowledgeable Oriental Bahá'í teachers (including Abu'l-Fadl). At the same time, Kheiralla broke with 'Abdu'l-Bahá and transferred his allegiance to Muhammad-'Alí. A small number of Americans followed his example – calling themselves 'Behaists' – but the majority of the Bahá'ís remained loyal to 'Abdu'l-Bahá.

After 1900, the North American Bahá'í community grew very slowly until the impetus of 'Abdu'l-Bahá's visit (April to December 1912). It revealed a considerable internal dynamism, however, with the development of a substantial body of Bahá'í literature, including English-language translations of writings by Bahá'u'lláh and 'Abdu'l-Bahá, accounts of pilgrimage visits to 'Abdu'l-Bahá by American Bahá'ís, and introductory pamphlets and books on the Faith written for a Christian readership. A project to plan for the construction of a Bahá'í House of Worship near Chicago was also begun, with the establishment of an annual national delegate convention of American Bahá'ís (the Baha'i Temple Unity) in 1909. With 'Abdu'l-Bahá's encouragement a variety of local Bahá'í councils also came into being.

American Bahá'ís were also extremely active internationally. A number were able to make the lengthy journey to visit 'Abdu'l-Bahá in the Holy Land. Others visited the Bahá'ís in the Middle East, India and Central Asia, including some who settled in Iran to help with medical and educational work among Bahá'ís. Yet others became missionary teachers, establishing the Faith in Hawaii (1901), Germany (from 1905), Japan (from 1914), Australia (1920) and Brazil (1921). Others made extensive tours to teach the Faith in Latin America, the Yukon and Southern Africa.

Growth outside the United States was slight. Active Bahá'í groups formed in France, England and Germany, but their numbers remained small, despite 'Abdu'l-Bahá twice visiting Europe. Several of the European Bahá'ís were able to make major contributions to the development of the Faith, notably in terms of its literature, including works that are still among the most widely used introductory books on the Bahá'í Faith in French and English: *Essai sur le Béhaïsme* (1908) by Hippolyte Dreyfus, and *Bahá'u'lláh and the New Era* (1923) by John Esslemont.

Part Three

THE BAHÁ'Í FAITH SINCE 1922

'Abdu'l-Bahá and Shoghi Effendi in Haifa

Shoghi Effendi

Shoghi Effendi Rabbání was the eldest son of 'Abdu'l-Bahá's daughter, Díyá'iyyih Khánum (d. 1951) and Mírzá Hádí Shírází (d. 1955), a member of the extended family of the Báb's mother (the Afnáns). Shoghi Effendi was born in 'Akká on 1 March 1897, the eldest of 'Abdu'l-Bahá's thirteen grandchildren, and named in the latter's will as his successor when he was still a child.

He was apparently a boisterous but sensitive child, and was enormously attached to his grandfather. Educated at first at home with the other children of the household, he was later sent to Catholic schools in Haifa and Beirut (where he was very unhappy) and then to the Syrian Protestant College (the predecessor of the American University in Beirut, which he enjoyed), spending his summer holidays as one of his grandfather's assistants. He gained an arts degree from the college in 1918, and became 'Abdu'l-Bahá's chief secretary. Then in 1920 he went to Oxford University (Balliol College), where he studied political science and economics, and also sought to perfect his English so as to be better able to translate Bahá'í literature into that language. He was still in the midst of his studies when summoned to return to Haifa at the news of his grandfather's death.

The terms of 'Abdu'l-Bahá's will were explicit. Shoghi Effendi was to be 'Guardian of the Cause of God' (*Valí amru'lláh*, a title immediately reminiscent of Shí'í Imáms). He was the 'Centre of the Cause' and the 'sign of God' on earth. All should show 'their obedience, submissiveness and subordination' to him. He was also to be the head of the (as yet unelected) Universal House of Justice, and with it was under the unerring guidance and protection of Bahá'u'lláh and the Báb. As with it, obedience to him was the same as obedience to God and opposition to him the same as opposition to God, meriting divine vengeance. If they were worthy, the first-born of his lineal descendants should succeed him as Guardian. The original line of succession, indicated in Bahá'u'lláh's *Book of Covenant*, was put aside, 'Abdu'l-Bahá's half-brother, Muhammad-'Alí, having been 'cut off from the Holy Tree' as a result of his misdeeds.

The early years of Shoghi Effendi's Guardianship, up to the early 1930s, were characterized by two dominant themes: the establishment of his own position as centre of the Bahá'í Cause, and the systematization and extension of the Bahá'í administrative order.

For the vast majority of Bahá'ís, Shoghi Effendi's accession was greatly welcomed. After 'Abdu'l-Bahá's passing, he provided a new focal point to whom they might turn, and in addition to the obedience called for in 'Abdu'l-Bahá's testament, many were happy to accord him much the same devotion as they had shown to his grandfather. Shoghi Effendi had a clear vision of the future progress of the Cause and, through his meetings with pilgrims, as well as through thousands of letters, he shared this with the Bahá'ís and seems to have been readily able to inspire them. Unlike 'Abdu'l-Bahá, however, he never journeyed to visit the Bahá'ís abroad.

There was a clear contrast with 'Abdu'l-Bahá's leadership, and Shoghi Effendi himself sought to emphasize the difference. Abdu'l-Bahá had been a venerable, patriarchal figure; Shoghi Effendi was a young man of twenty-four, Western-educated and, apart from the black fez he usually wore, Western in dress. To the Bahá'ís, he signed his letters 'your true brother', and referred to the institution of the Guardianship rather than to his own personal role. The contrast was even greater with regard to the surrounding Palestinian society. 'Abdu'l-Bahá had acted as a local notable, even attending the mosque. Shoghi Effendi distanced himself from local notability and concentrated his energies on the worldwide direction of the Faith.

Shoghi Effendi's youth and the contrast between his style of leadership and that of 'Abdu'l-Bahá drew some negative responses, although their extent is difficult to judge. Certainly, some of the local British administrators initially referred to him disparagingly as 'the boy', and there were a small number of older Bahá'ís who appear to have adopted a patronizing attitude towards him, disapproving of his style and policies.

There was little in the way of outright opposition, however. And apart from an unsuccessful campaign by Muhammad-'Alí and his followers to gather support in the period following 'Abdu'l-Bahá's death, the only real challenges to his leadership were mounted in the late 1920s and early 1930s in the United States by Ruth White and Ahmad Sohrab, both of whom disapproved of Shoghi Effendi's emphasis on the authority of the Bahá'í administration. White was an American journalist who began a sustained campaign to attempt to prove that Shoghi Effendi had forged his grandfather's will. She attracted a small number of Western supporters, particularly in Germany, but Eastern Bahá'ís (including Sohrab), who were familiar with 'Abdu'l-Bahá's original writings and handwriting, found her claims spurious. For his part, Sohrab objected to the policies of the new American Bahá'í assembly and founded his own organization (the New History Society/the International Caravan of East and West) to further elements of the Bahá'í teachings.

Neither White nor Sohrab was able to gain many followers.

Shoghi Effendi himself took a number of years to come to terms with his appointment as Guardian. He faced a mass of work and many problems in his new role. Already greatly shocked by 'Abdu'l-Bahá's death, he repeatedly worked himself to a state of nervous exhaustion and collapse, necessitating several extended absences from Haifa during the first few years of his Guardianship. His work continued, however. In addition to his extensive correspondence (over 17,500 letters by him or his secretary collected to date) which involved detailed monitoring of the situation of all Bahá'í communities, he was able to complete a number of translations of Bahá'í literature (mostly the writings of Bahá'u'lláh), organize responses to attacks on the Faith in the Middle East, and pursue his plans for regularizing Bahá'í administration, for the global expansion of the Faith, and for the development of the Bahá'í World Centre in Haifa–'Akká.

Shoghi Effendi's personal life was generally uneventful and was largely subordinated to his work as Guardian. The problem of securing sufficient secretarial support to help with the ever-growing mass of correspondence was only really resolved in the 1950s, by which time Shoghi Effendi had long since adjusted to a pattern of unremitting hard work when in Haifa, interspersing this with summer breaks during which he visited Europe – in the early years usually going to the Swiss Alps – and on two occasions he travelled through Africa from south to north (1929 and 1940).

He enjoyed good relations with the official representatives of the British and later the Israeli administrations, and apart from the possibility of Nazi occupation during World War II and the troubled period during which the new state of Israel was being established, there was no external threat to his position or his work. And apart from White, Sohrab and a few isolated individuals in Iran, there was no significant opposition within the Faith.

In 1937 he married Mary Maxwell (b. 1910), the only daughter of two North American Bahá'ís. The couple had no children, but Rúhíyyih Khánum, as she was titled, became his helpmate and constant companion until his passing in 1957. During the 1940s, a conflict developed between Shoghi Effendi and many members of his extended family (his brother, sisters, cousins and aunts), partly because of their contacts, including marriage, with Covenant-breaking members of Bahá'u'lláh's extended family. All were eventually excommunicated by him.

Writings and Translations

Shoghi Effendi had originally gone to Oxford to perfect his English in order to serve as a translator of Bahá'í literature. He retained a great love of the English language (together with a mild Oxford accent) and was as comfortable in his use of English as in the Persian and Arabic of his childhood. He also spoke French. Although the vast majority of his writings are letters (mostly in Persian or English), he found time during his Guardianship to complete a number of translations as well as to write one book, a lengthy history of the Faith, *God Passes By* (1944).

Shoghi Effendi's letters range from routine correspondence dealing with the activities of Bahá'ís in various parts of the world to lengthy monographs addressing specific themes. Some of the letters dealing with routine matters were written on his behalf by a secretary. These he then read through, often adding a personal postscript offering encouragement or direction. To date, fifteen volumes of the English-language letters have been published: collections of more or less routine letters to the American, Canadian, Alaskan, British, German, Indian, Australian and New

Zealand Bahá'ís, together with monograph letters on the 'World Order of Bahá'u'lláh', the teaching of the Bahá'í Faith (*The Advent of Divine Justice*), and Bahá'u'lláh's proclamation to the rulers (*The Promised Day Is Come*). Published copies of other letters are found in various compilations. Some of his letters to the Iranian Bahá'ís have also been published in the original, but these are generally difficult to obtain, and few have been translated.

The letters cover a variety of themes: encouragement to the Bahá'ís to teach and to endeavour to live the life of true Bahá'ís; reports of Bahá'í activities in various parts of the world, commonly pointing to the wider significance of particular events; calls to the believers to achieve specific goals such as the settlement of Bahá'ís in new lands, the establishment of assemblies, the translation of Bahá'í literature, and the acquisition of Bahá'í centres and other properties; analysis of particular developments within Bahá'í history; statements about Bahá'í beliefs, morality, social principles, law and administration; and obituaries of outstanding Bahá'ís.

As Shoghi Effendi himself emphasized, 'Abdu'l-Bahá had conferred upon the Guardianship the function of 'interpreter of the word of God' (*World Order* 148, 150–1). As such, Guardians were empowered 'to reveal the purport and disclose the implications of the utterances of Bahá'u'lláh and of 'Abdu'l-Bahá' (*World Order* 151). These interpretations were authoritative and binding.

In this regard, Shoghi Effendi's 'World Order' letters (1929–36) have particular importance. One, 'The Dispensation of Bahá'u'lláh' (8 February 1934), is a major doctrinal statement in which Shoghi Effendi delineates the religious 'stations' of the central figures of the Bahá'í Faith (Bahá'u'lláh, the Báb and 'Abdu'l-Bahá) as well as the role of the Guardianship and the Universal House of Justice as the primary institutions of the Bahá'í administrative order. Several other letters – notably 'The

Goal of a New World Order' (28 November 1931) and 'The Unfoldment of World Civilization' (11 March 1936) – place the worsening economic and political situation of the 1930s in the context of Bahá'u'lláh's summons to establish the Most Great Peace, outlining the guiding principles of Bahá'u'lláh's world order and referring to an 'age of transition' in human history heralding the emergence of a new age and eventually a world civilization. There is also his statement 'The Faith of Bahá'u'lláh' (1947), addressed to the United Nations Palestine Committee, in which he outlines the fundamentals of the Bahá'í Faith.

Of Shoghi Effendi's translations, a few short pieces appeared in print in the 1920s, together with a collaborative rendering of Bahá'u'lláh's *The Hidden Words*. Then, between 1931 and 1941, he published four volumes of Bahá'u'lláh's writings, together with a translation of Nabíl's history of the Bábís, which appeared in English under the title *The Dawn-Breakers* (1932). Many other passages translated from Bahá'í scripture appeared in his letters.

Development of the Administrative Order

Elements of the Bahá'í administrative system had been described or established by Bahá'u'lláh and 'Abdu'l-Bahá, but it was only during the period of Shoghi Effendi's Guardianship that a complete system of administration emerged, increasingly replacing the more personalized and informal patterns of local leadership and organization that had previously prevailed.

There were two separate periods of administrative development. In the first, in the 1920s, Shoghi Effendi regularized and extended the system of elected spiritual assemblies. The basic elements were laid out in 1922 and 1923. All Bahá'í groups in which there were at least nine adults (aged twenty-one and above) were called upon to form their own local spiritual assemblies, each assembly superintending all Bahá'í activities in its locality. In all 'national' communities in which there were a sufficient number of Bahá'ís, national spiritual assemblies were to be elected by a delegate convention. Both local and national assemblies were to establish their own funds and the necessary committees to help them in their work of promoting Bahá'í teaching endeavour, publishing, and organizing the community life of the Bahá'ís. There were subsequent elaborations of detail, but in its key aspects, the system has not changed to the present day.

Other administrative developments from the 1920s included the delineation of specific requirements for voting membership of the Bahá'í community, and the establishment of national administrative centres, each overseen by the elected secretary of the relevant national spiritual assembly. The secretaryship became, in some cases, a full-time occupation. Membership rolls were also introduced, along with enrolment cards to record professions of faith, and credential cards or letters to indicate membership. Regular 'nineteen day feasts', held at the beginning of each Bahá'í month, were strongly emphasized and came to include a period of consultation on local Bahá'í activities and assembly directives. Wherever possible, the national and local assemblies secured some form of legal identity, enabling them to own property.

The overall effect of these developments was to create a far more tightly organized network of Bahá'í communities. Organization came to be a central element in Bahá'í community life, and it was invested with spiritual and moral importance. Levels of administrative functioning varied, of course, but by the 1930s a generally efficient system was in place, with the establishment of local and national spiritual assemblies becoming one of the major goals of Bahá'í activity as well as a significant measure of Bahá'í expansion (see below).

The second period of administrative development took place in the 1950s, and comprised the creation or reanimation of three separate institutions:

1. The International Bahá'í Council (1950/1–63), initially an appointed (later elected) body, charged with assisting Shoghi Effendi in his work in Haifa. It was also seen as the precursor of the Universal House of Justice.

2. The Hands of the Cause of God, an institution revived in 1951 as a functioning group of senior Bahá'ís, was responsible for assisting the national spiritual assemblies to achieve their goals, and involved with the protection of the Faith from external and internal attacks. An initial group of twelve was increased to twenty-seven by 1957, comprising individuals in all continents and including several members of the first International Council.

3. The Auxiliary Boards, whose members were to act as the 'deputies, assistants and advisers' to the Hands. Two Boards were established, each organized on a continental level: one concerned with the propagation and expansion of the Faith (1954), and a second with its protection (1957).

All these institutions included both men and women.

Systematic Teaching Plans

In his *Tablets of the Divine Plan*, 'Abdu'l-Bahá had called for a systematic endeavour to teach the Faith throughout the world. Several individuals had responded to his appeal, but no sustained expansion had resulted. During the 1920s, Shoghi Effendi often reminded the Bahá'ís of the importance of teaching, but it was only as the system of assemblies began to function effectively that he started to implement his grandfather's summons for global expansion. The assemblies were to be the agency whereby an increasingly lengthy list of objectives was to be achieved: 'pioneers' were sent to open new countries and territories to the Faith, new assemblies were established, Bahá'í literature was translated and published, and properties such as Bahá'í centres were acquired.

The most important Bahá'í community in this regard was that of the United States and Canada. Larger and better organized than any other Western Bahá'í community then established, it also possessed a religious freedom and access to material resources unavailable to Bahá'í communities of the East. It was to North America, then, that the first systematic teaching plan was assigned: a Seven Year Plan (1937–44), in which the Bahá'ís were called upon to settle Bahá'í 'pioneers' in all the American states, Canadian provinces and Latin American republics in which there were as yet no Bahá'ís. They were also to continue working towards the completion of the Bahá'í House of Worship at Wilmette, Chicago.

This plan became the model for a series of future plans, both in North America and elsewhere. In a second Seven Year Plan (1946–53), the Americans were directed to promote Bahá'í expansion throughout the Americas and also to re-establish and consolidate the Faith in Europe after the devastation of World War II. They were also to ensure the final completion of the Wilmette Temple and, as part of their work in the Americas, to establish a new independent national spiritual assembly for the Canadian Bahá'ís, as well as two large regional assemblies, one for South America and one for Central America and the Antilles.

All the other national assemblies were also given goals, or in some cases set their own. These included the reinforcement of their own 'home fronts' through increasing their geographical extent and the number of their local assemblies. In the case of the stronger assemblies, they also included an international component. The Iranian and Egyptian Bahá'ís were required to establish new Bahá'í groups in the Middle East and North Africa, the Indians were to settle pioneers in South-East Asia, and the British were to co-ordinate a project involving several national assemblies to establish the Faith in various African territories (1951–3). The new Canadian and Latin American assemblies were also assigned goals.

The results of these various national plans were highly encouraging, and in 1953, all twelve national assemblies then in existence embarked on a ten-year 'Global Crusade', designed by Shoghi Effendi to secure the establishment of the Faith throughout the world. The designated goals were in many cases exceeded, and not only was there a massive geographical expansion, but in several areas of the world there was a large-scale influx of new Bahá'ís (see chapter 11).

Some indication of the expansion that resulted from these plans can be gained from the following statistics. In 1935, before the first of the national plans, 139 local spiritual assemblies had been established worldwide, and there were Bahá'ís living in 1,034 localities. By 1953, at the start of the Ten Year Crusade, these figures had increased to 670 and 2,700 respectively, and by 1963, at the Crusade's completion, to 4,437 and 14,437 (Smith, 'Expansion and distribution'). Over the same period, the number of national assemblies increased from ten in 1935, to twelve in 1953, and to fifty-six by 1963.

Other significant developments were the construction of Bahá'í Houses of Worship at Kampala, Uganda and Sydney,

Australia (both dedicated for worship in 1961), and increasing contact with the United Nations (1948–; see chapter 10).

The Bahá'í World Centre

The initial development of the Bahá'í 'World Centre' in the Haifa–'Akká area was also largely the work of Shoghi Effendi. This involved a number of separate projects. In the 'Akká area, he obtained the mansion of Bahá'u'lláh at Bahjí in 1929 and began an extensive renovation. Later, during the 1950s, he secured legal possession of the surrounding lands and created a number of gardens and installed ornamental lighting. He also renovated the house in which Bahá'u'lláh had spent most of his years in 'Akká, and obtained possession of other sites associated with Bahá'u'lláh. In Haifa, he extended the shrine complex in which the Báb and 'Abdu'l-Bahá were interred (1929), and had an elaborate golden-domed superstructure built to envelop the shrine (1948–53). He also purchased the surrounding lands and created gardens, again with ornamental lighting. Above the shrine, a Parthenon-like International Archives building was constructed to house Bahá'í relics and scriptures (1955–7), the two buildings together with the gardens becoming a major Haifa landmark.

The Hands of the Cause, 1957–63

Shoghi Effendi died unexpectedly on 4 November 1957 during a visit to London, and was buried there. Two weeks later the Hands of the Cause met together in their first conclave in Haifa. A search of Shoghi Effendi's sealed room was made, but no will was found, and it became evident that he had not appointed a successor nor left any guidance as to what should now be done. In his

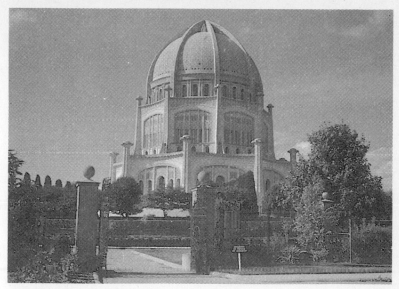

Bahá'í Temple in Wilmette, USA

Bahá'í Temple in Kampala, Uganda

Bahá'í Temple in Sydney, Australia

The International Archives Building and the shrine of the Báb

last general letter to the Bahá'ís, in October 1957, he had, however, referred to the Hands as 'the Chief Stewards of Bahá'u'lláh's embryonic World Commonwealth', who had been invested with 'the dual function of guarding over the security, and of ensuring the propagation of [the] Faith' (*Messages* 127). This statement provided them with the legal basis to assume headship of the Faith.

The Hands retained this headship until 1963 when, on their instructions, the elections for the first Universal House of Justice were held. The Hands debarred themselves from election to the House. The appointed International Bahá'í Council had meanwhile been replaced by an elected council (1961), the electors for both the International Council (disbanded 1963) and the Universal House of Justice being the members of all national spiritual assemblies. As the House of Justice was guaranteed divine support and guidance in the Bahá'í writings, its election came as a major psychological reassurance to both the Hands and the Bahá'í world as a whole.

The Bahá'í world largely accepted the temporary custodial role of the Hands. The exception was one of the most senior of the American Hands, Charles Mason Remey, who proclaimed himself second Guardian of the Faith in 1960 and succeeded in attracting a small but widely spread following of Bahá'ís. The rest of the Hands and the overwhelming majority of the Bahá'í world rejected these claims, and Remey and his followers were subsequently declared Covenant-breakers.

After Remey's death in 1974, his followers split into several mutually antagonistic groups. A small remnant is still active, mainly in the United States.

The Universal House of Justice

The Universal House of Justice was first elected in April 1963 and ever since has acted as the supreme administrative body in the Bahá'í world. One of its earliest pronouncements (October 1963) was that there was no way in which any further Guardians could be appointed in succession to Shoghi Effendi (*Wellspring of Guidance* 11), and it has thus also assumed permanent headship of the Faith. The absence of a Guardian represented a 'grievous loss', but the continued unity and guidance of the Faith under the direction of the House of Justice is regarded as divinely assured.

The system used to elect the Universal House of Justice was established by 'Abdu'l-Bahá: namely, by the collected votes of the members of all existing national spiritual assemblies (fifty-six in 1963, 165 in 1993). Other aspects of the House's functioning have been determined by the House itself and confirmed in its adopted constitution (26 November 1972). Thus, there are at present nine members; elections are held every five years at an international convention of national assembly members (to date all held in Haifa); and the House has no officers, but otherwise conducts its affairs much as the spiritual assemblies do. In keeping with the instruction of 'Abdu'l-Bahá – and in contrast to all other present Bahá'í bodies – the membership is confined to men.

Although greatly respected, the members of the House do not have any special status or authority within the Faith as individuals. It is as a collectivity that the House exercises its leadership. To date, a total of sixteen men have served as members of the House. The membership has been highly stable, the only changes of membership having occurred as a result of death or retirement. Of the original nine members elected in 1963, three still serve. By national origins, five of the members have been Iranians from outside Iran, eight have been North Americans, two British and one Australian. The members clearly cultivate an ethos of individual self-effacement.

There have been no significant internal challenges to the leadership of the House, and whilst some of the Remeyite groups remain active, Covenant-breaking has been quiescent during the thirty years since its election.

Writings, Compilations and Translations

The Universal House of Justice is empowered to legislate on matters not revealed in the Bahá'í scriptures. Up to the present time, however, it has been extremely limited in its exercise of this function. Instead, it has preferred to provide directive guidance to the Bahá'ís in its role as head of the Faith and to collect and publish a large mass of extracts from the writings of Bahá'u'lláh, the Báb, 'Abdu'l-Bahá and Shoghi Effendi.

As with Shoghi Effendi, the House's guidance has taken the form of letters to Bahá'í communities, institutions and individuals, and sometimes to the entire Bahá'í world. Three volumes of these letters have been published so far, and many more are found in Bahá'í periodicals. The letters are regarded as divinely empowered. Compilations of Bahá'í writings on a wide range of subjects have been produced, including various aspects of Bahá'í administration, teaching, prayer, music, education and family life. Translations of writings by Bahá'u'lláh, the Báb and 'Abdu'l-Bahá have also been

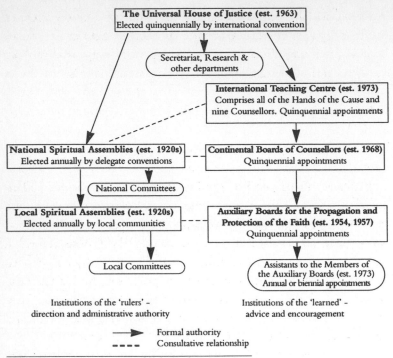

The present-day structure of Bahá'í administration

commissioned, including most recently Bahá'u'lláh's book of laws, the *Kitáb-i-Aqdas* (1992). In addition to its messages addressed to the Bahá'ís, the House has also published its own constitution (1972), prepared a volume of Bahá'u'lláh's letters to the kings for presentation to contemporary heads of state (1967), and issued a call to 'the peoples of the world' to respond to the Bahá'í teachings on the establishment of universal peace (*The Promise of World Peace*, 1985).

This work has necessitated the establishment of research and archival departments in Haifa. Of the letters of Bahá'u'lláh, Abdu'l-Bahá and Shoghi Effendi, over 60,000 items had already been collected by 1983. An extensive programme of preservation, classification and indexing is still in progress. These collected writings give the House a massive amount of data on which to base its deliberations and an ever-increasing body of published scripture and authoritative interpretation for all Bahá'ís.

Administration

The major developments in Bahá'í administration since 1963 concern the 'institutions of the learned' and the Bahá'í World Centre in Haifa. Bahá'u'lláh had referred to 'the rulers' and 'the learned' in the Faith, terms which have come to refer respectively to the elected assemblies, and the Hands of the Cause and their assistants. In the absence of a living Guardian, the House of Justice ruled in November 1964 that there was no longer a way to appoint further Hands. Therefore, in order for the Hands' vital functions of fostering the expansion of the Faith and protecting it from the attacks of its opponents to be continued into the future, the House created new institutions: Continental Boards of Counsellors (established in 1968, now with seventy-two members on five Boards), who would take over the work of the Hands on a continental basis, including the direction of the Auxiliary Boards; and an International Teaching Centre in Haifa (established in 1973), to direct the Continental and Auxiliary Boards, and on which the remaining Hands would also serve. The number of Auxiliary Board members was also greatly increased (from seventy-two in 1957 to 846 in 1992), and they were empowered to appoint their own assistants to help them with their work.

The House has also greatly expanded the staff at the Bahá'í World Centre, responding both to the increasing extent of the Bahá'í community globally and the increasing range of work the House directs or initiates. Thus, in addition to its secretariat, financial and maintenance departments (the latter for the Bahá'í shrines, gardens and other buildings), it has created a public information office, an office of social and economic development, and various other agencies. Instead of the handful of staff employed under Shoghi Effendi, there are now several hundred.

Systematic Planning

Shoghi Effendi established a framework of systematic planning to achieve stated objectives, and this has been continued and developed by the Universal House of Justice. To date, there have been five international plans launched by the House: the Nine (1964–73), Five (1974–9), Seven (1979–86), Six (1986–92), and Three (1993–6) Year Plans. In general format these have resembled Shoghi Effendi's Ten Year Crusade, albeit with a wider range of goals. A subsidiary two-year plan (1990–2) co-ordinated Bahá'í activity in Eastern Europe and the former Soviet Union under the new conditions of religious freedom that followed the collapse of the communist regimes there.

Plan objectives have included worldwide expansion and consolidation goals, which by 1992 involved some 165 national spiritual assemblies in the detailed process of preparation. The results of these endeavours have been impressive. Between 1963 and 1992, the total number of localities in the world in which Bahá'ís reside increased from 14,000 to over 120,000, whilst the number of local spiritual assemblies increased from 4,437 to 20,435. There has also been an enormous increase in the number of languages into which Bahá'í literature has been translated (in excess of 800 languages by 1988), and the continued acquisition or construction of national and local Bahá'í centres.

Of particular significance in terms of buildings has been the construction of more Bahá'í Houses of Worship. In 1963 there

Bahá'í Temple in Frankfurt, Germany

Bahá'í Temple in New Delhi, India

were only three (Wilmette, Kampala and Sydney), but these have since been augmented by Temples in Frankfurt, Germany (1964), Panama City (1972), Apia, Western Samoa (1984), and New Delhi, India (1986). Often reflecting indigenous architectural styles, these buildings have served as 'silent teachers' of the Faith, the New Delhi Temple in particular attracting thousands of visitors every day.

To achieve the goals of expansion and consolidation, the Universal House of Justice has sought to extend both the processes of planning and the available resources. Thus all local as well as national assemblies are now encouraged to develop their own goals as part of their respective national plans; neighbouring national communities have been encouraged to develop joint projects, as for example teaching along their common borders; and many national assemblies have been assigned specific collaboration goals (with, for example, a richer community funding a capital project in a poorer community), so that a web of interconnections between Bahá'í communities has been created. A multitude of Bahá'í pioneers and travel teachers has settled in or visited other countries to help establish or deepen new Bahá'í communities, and increasing emphasis has been placed on tapping the energies and time of young Bahá'ís in their teens and twenties, whose endeavours have contributed markedly to the rapid growth of Bahá'í communities worldwide.

One aspect of expansion that has assumed major importance is the attempt to proclaim the Bahá'í teachings to the generality of the world's population. This has involved establishing contacts with prominent people and the media, and also grassroots campaigns of 'mass teaching'. In some countries such teaching has been remarkably successful and large numbers of new Bahá'ís – including many poorly educated villagers in the Third World – have entered the Faith. Considerable attention has been given to ways

The Seat of the Universal House of Justice

in which these believers can be properly integrated into the Bahá'í community, such as by creating village teaching institutes and, particularly in Latin America, by broadcasts from Bahá'í radio stations.

In addition to these essentially quantitative goals, the Universal House has also sought to develop qualitative aspects of Bahá'í community life, including enhancing the role of women; fostering Bahá'í family life, education and literacy; and increasing the administrative efficiency of assemblies and committees. It has aimed to increase the sense of global community among Bahá'ís by holding large-scale international Bahá'í conferences in various parts of the world. Notable among these were the two world congresses, the first in London organized by the Hands but held just after the election of the House in 1963, and the second, attended by around 27,000 people from 180 countries, in New York in 1992.

The Further Development of the Bahá'í World Centre

Like Shoghi Effendi, the House of Justice has worked to secure ownership of sites associated with the central figures of the faith – such as the house in which 'Abdu'l-Bahá lived in 'Akká – and to extend and beautify the gardens surrounding the Bahá'í shrines in Haifa and Bahjí. More dramatic, however, has been its construction of a large stately building to serve as its own seat in Haifa (1975–83) and the extensive project recently begun to build centres for the study of texts and for the International Teaching Centre along an arc on Mount Carmel. A large library is also projected.

Social Issues

The Bahá'í teachings advocate a thorough reconstruction of human society, but until recently practical work to implement a new social order has been largely confined to certain areas of

Bahá'í community life, particularly education and the ongoing endeavour to free Bahá'ís from all forms of racial and religious prejudice so as to foster a genuinely unified community. Otherwise, Bahá'í activity has been more concerned with the expansion and administrative consolidation of the Faith.

This situation has changed quite dramatically in recent years, partly no doubt in response to the material needs of the large numbers of new Bahá'ís in the poor rural areas of the Third World. By the 1970s there was an increasing number of local Bahá'í initiatives in literacy training, health education and rural development. In 1983, the House of Justice established a Haifa-based Office of Social and Economic Development to provide a greater measure of international co-ordination and co-operation. Local development programmes have since pro-liferated. Like earlier educational and medical projects in Iran, these are generally non-sectarian in orientation and are geared to the whole community, not just to the Bahá'ís. They include a wide range of educational facilities, from village tutorial schools teaching basic literacy to a Bahá'í university (in Bolivia, 1985); rural health schemes; and institutes to train and empower rural women. The emphasis has been on human resources and communal self-development rather than on major financial investment.

In addition to material development, the Bahá'ís have also concerned themselves with cultural matters, most particularly in parts of Latin America where they have contributed to the life of Amerindian cultures, as with the use of Bahá'í radio stations to foster indigenous music.

Another aspect of this more socially activist stance is the major emphasis placed by the House of Justice on Bahá'í involve-ment with environmental issues. Bahá'ís played a prominent part in the 'Earth Summit' in Rio de Janeiro in 1992 and were the only religious non-governmental organization to make a formal presentation to it. Also of note is the recent establishment of the European Bahá'í Business Forum (1990), which among other activities has organized conferences on business ethics.

Another Bahá'í activity that has now assumed far greater prominence is the public advocacy of the peace programme represented by the teachings of Bahá'u'lláh and 'Abdu'l-Bahá. This was given great emphasis in 1985 with the publication of *The Promise of World Peace* by the Universal House of Justice. Addressed 'to the peoples of the world', the statement was extensively distributed, including formal presentations to many public figures. Insisting on the imperative necessity of working towards peace on the lines of the Bahá'í programme, the House also pointed to the present positive trends towards greater global and regional unity and to the increased concern with peace issues among non-governmental organizations and others. It also warned against the destructive impact of despair and the uncritical acceptance of human aggression as a supposedly natural trait.

A similar document, *The Prosperity of Humankind*, describing those elements of social development that are conducive to the material and spiritual advance of civilization, was released recently (1995).

Involvement with the United Nations

During the Guardianship of Shoghi Effendi, contacts between the Bahá'ís and both the League of Nations and the United Nations had been actively encouraged. An International Bahá'í Bureau was established to liaise with the former (1925), and a body representative of all the then existing national spiritual assemblies, the 'Bahá'í International Community', was affiliated with the United Nations in 1948.

Bahá'í involvement with the UN and its agencies increased enormously from the 1960s onwards, reflecting the growing numerical strength of the Bahá'í community internationally as well as its increasing concern with development issues. The persecution of the Bahá'ís in Iran since 1979 has also done much to deepen Bahá'í links with the UN. The enhancement of the Bahá'í relationship with the United Nations has been a continuing objective of the Universal House of Justice, which has encouraged grassroots Bahá'í support for various UN projects as well as making a number of initiatives through the Bahá'í International Community (BIC).

A permanent Bahá'í office was established at the UN in New York in 1967. Since then, the BIC has gained consultative status as a non-governmental organization with the UN's Economic and Social Council (ECOSOC, 1970) and Children's Fund (UNICEF, 1976), as well as working relationships with various other UN bodies. It has also established a second office in Geneva and become extensively involved with UN work relating to literacy, human rights, primary health care, combating racism and women's issues. Offices of the BIC concerned with public information (1985), the environment (1989), and the advancement of women (1992) have also been established.

The persecution of Bahá'ís in several countries has also been brought before the UN and international action has been brought to bear. This has been most marked in relation to the massive persecution of the Bahá'ís in Iran following the establishment of an Islamic revolutionary regime in 1979. UN pressure has been directed towards the Iranian government to prevent attacks on the Bahá'ís, seemingly with success.

Bahá'í UN contacts have also led to increasing collaboration with other non-governmental organizations such as the World Wide Fund for Nature Network on Conservation and Religion and the 'Advocates for African Food Security: Lessening the Burden for Women', of which the BIC was a founding member. Such collaboration is necessarily restricted, however, by the Bahá'ís' insistence on remaining uninvolved in partisan political issues.

Bahá'í Communities, 1922 to the Present

Bahá'u'lláh regarded himself as the promised redeemer for the whole human race. His message was universal. During Bahá'u'lláh's own lifetime, however, the Bahá'í Faith remained confined to a largely Islamic Middle Eastern milieu, and it was not until the ministry of 'Abdu'l-Bahá that this situation began to change, largely through the establishment of Bahá'í communities in the West. This represented a very significant internationalization of the Faith, but the actual number of Bahá'ís did not greatly increase and Iranians remained in the majority.

During the ministry of Shoghi Effendi, the actual diffusion of Bahá'ís in the world greatly increased as a result of the national teaching plans he initiated (1937–53). There was a growth in numbers, but, until the early 1950s, the total number of Bahá'ís outside Iran remained minute: perhaps 13,000 in all (Smith and Momen, 'The Bahá'í Faith 1957–1988' 70), with the USA being the only other country having a Bahá'í community of even modest size. This stage in the Faith's development continued essentially until the Ten Year Crusade (1953–63). The Iranian Bahá'í community also grew, but by natural increase rather than new conversions, and by the 1950s was probably in the region of 200,000.

Since the 1950s, however, the situation has changed significantly and the Bahá'í Faith has begun to assume the dimensions of a world religion, albeit still small in size. Central to this

Table 1: Local Spiritual Assemblies (LSAs) and localities in which Bahá'ís reside: 1949, 1964 and 1992

Geographical Areas	1949		1964		1992	
	LSAs	Localities	LSAs	Localities	LSAs	Localities
The Islamic Heartland	304 (51.0)[a]	777 (33.8)	594 (13.1)	1,679 (11.1)	162 (0.8)	1,396 (1.2)
Iran	281 (47.1)	709 (30.8)	530 (11.6)	1,503 (9.9)	0 (0.0)[b]	709 (0.6)
Middle East and North Africa (excl. Iran)	22 (3.7)	66 (2.9)	52 (1.1)	136 (0.9)	88 (0.4)	349 (0.3)
Central Asia, Caucasus and Turkey	1 (0.2)	2 (0.1)	12 (0.3)	40 (0.3)	74 (0.4)	338 (0.3)
The West	222 (37.2)	1,352 (58.8)	637 (13.9)	2,959 (19.5)	2,979 (14.6)	13,133 (10.8)
North America	171 (28.7)	1,207 (52.5)	414 (9.0)	2,044 (13.5)	1,890 (9.3)	8,530 (7.1)
Anglo-Pacific	12 (2.0)	19 (0.8)	39 (0.9)	176 (1.2)	255 (1.2)	530 (0.4)
Western Europe	39 (6.5)	125 (5.4)	182 (4.0)	726 (4.8)	708 (3.5)	3,273 (2.7)
The Balkans, Eastern Europe and Russia	0 (0.0)	1 (0.0)	2 (0.0)	13 (0.1)	126 (0.6)	800 (0.7)

The Bahá'í Third World

Sub-Saharan Africa	70 (11.7)	171 (7.4)	3,347 (73.1)	10,547 (69.5)	17,287 (84.6)	105,508 (87.9)
Latin America and the Caribbean	1 (0.2)	8 (0.3)	1,327 (29.0)	3,173 (20.9)	5,877 (28.8)	33,040 (27.5)
South Asia	35 (5.9)	70 (3.0)	294 (5.4)	1,456 (9.6)	3,501 (17.1)	18,940 (15.8)
South-East Asia	28 (4.7)	69 (3.0)	1,111 (24.3)	4,651 (30.6)	5,676 (27.8)	37,086 (30.9)
East Asia	5 (0.8)	15 (0.7)	543 (11.9)	905 (6.0)	1,426 (7.0)	11,671 (9.7)
Oceania	1 (0.2)	7 (0.3)	29 (0.6)	126 (0.8)	193 (0.9)	1,207 (1.0)
	0 (0.0)	2 (0.1)	43 (0.9)	236 (1.6)	614 (3.0)	3,564 (3.0)
World Totals	**596**	**2,300**	**4,578**	**15,185**	**20,428**	**120,037**

Notes:

a Figures in parentheses represent the percentage of the world total.
b Bahá'í institutions in Iran were disbanded by government order in 1983.

Sources:

Calculated from *Bahá'í World*, Vol. XI, pp. 519–74; *Bahá'í World*, Vol. XIV, pp. 124–35; Universal House of Justice, Department of Statistics, 'Statistical Table, Six Year Plan Final Figures, 20 April 1992', mimeographed.

has been a new pattern of sustained and rapid growth. Beginning with the Ten Year Crusade, the Bahá'ís have been able to attract large numbers of new believers, so that the total number of followers worldwide is now in the region of five million. These include Bahá'í communities in almost every part of the world, a significant number of them large and well rooted. Of the five million Bahá'ís, only 300,000 or so live in Iran. From comprising well over ninety per cent of the total Bahá'í population until at least the 1950s, the Iranian Bahá'ís now represent perhaps only six to seven per cent. Even if we include the extensive Iranian diaspora, it is clearly no longer possible to regard the Bahá'í Faith in primarily Iranian terms.

The Bahá'í Faith has now expanded throughout the world, but the worldwide distribution of Bahá'ís is highly uneven. The distribution pattern has also changed markedly during recent years.

To describe these complexities it is useful to use a geo-cultural model of expansion. Until 1892, the Bahá'í Faith was still essentially confined to the Middle East and the Islamic world. Expansion in the West, beginning in 1894, represented a major cultural breakthrough and the beginning of the 'internationalization' of the Faith. There was then a slow process of establishing new Bahá'í centres in other parts of the world, but until the 1950s the Bahá'í Faith had in effect two axes: its traditional Islamic heartland centred on Iran, and a second 'world' centred on the American Bahá'í community but including small numbers of Europeans and other Westerners or those with a Western cultural background (such as members of the Latin American educated élite). Thus by the early 1950s, of the 13,000 or so Bahá'ís who lived outside the Middle East, 10,000 lived in the West (Smith and Momen, 'The Bahá'í Faith 1957–1988' 72). Similarly, by 1949, of 1,523 localities where Bahá'ís resided outside the Middle East,

1,207 were in North America, 145 were in Europe and the Pacific, and only 169 were in Latin America, sub-Saharan Africa and the rest of Asia combined (see table above).

This pattern has now changed dramatically, mainly because of a further cultural breakthrough into the largely rural masses of the Third World. Although diverse in their religious traditions and historical backgrounds, these peoples have shown a remarkable similarity of response to Bahá'í teaching. Their large numbers make them the predominant element in today's world Bahá'í community. Thus, of over 120,000 localities in which Bahá'ís resided in 1992, only one per cent were in the Faith's Islamic heartland, eleven per cent were in the West and eighty-eight per cent were in the rest of the world: thirty-one per cent in South Asia (mainly India), twenty-eight per cent in sub-Saharan Africa, sixteen per cent in Latin America and the Caribbean and ten per cent in South-East Asia (see table). Apart from greatly understating the presence of the Faith in the Middle East – where a renewal of persecution has led to a major contraction in the recorded number of localities in Iran – these figures give a good indication of the present distribution of Bahá'ís in the world.

The Islamic Heartland

Iran

After the collapse of Qájár rule in Iran, power was eventually consolidated in the hands of one of the army leaders who proclaimed himself as Reza Sháh in 1925 and established a new dynasty, the Pahlavis. This lasted until 1979, when it was overthrown and replaced by an Islamic republic. During the Pahlavi period, the government greatly increased the extent of centralized control over all elements of Iranian society and pursued policies of secular modernization and development.

For the Bahá'ís, Pahlavi rule at first seemed to offer an end to their sufferings, with the government limiting the power of the 'ulamá to incite persecution. Seeing themselves as agents for the revitalization of Iran, and opposed to clerical power, the Bahá'ís welcomed a regime that appeared to have similar objectives. The divergent aims of the government and the Bahá'ís were vividly illustrated in 1934, however, when the government ordered the closure of the prestigious Bahá'í schools (which were also attended by children from non-Bahá'í families). Independent institutions of any kind were suspect, and as the Bahá'ís offered what was in effect an alternative ideology of modernization, such schools were not to be encouraged. Neither were the Bahá'ís given any official recognition, and while individual Bahá'ís were co-opted to work for the regime in various capacities (including Muhammad Reza Sháh's doctor, for example), and the community as a whole was generally allowed to consolidate its institutions in private, the Bahá'ís lost the opportunities they had earlier enjoyed to present their beliefs openly to some sections of the Iranian public. Bahá'ís as individuals also suffered from their lack of civil status, being unable to contract legal marriages or validly complete government forms. Moreover, the government tolerated the development of well-organized anti-Bahá'í propaganda and secret societies to which the Bahá'ís had no means of reply. Government-sponsored persecution also occurred, most notably in 1955, when nation-wide anti-Bahá'í pogroms were encouraged, seemingly as a sop to right-wing Islamic groups.

In these circumstances, growth of the Bahá'í Faith in Iran beyond its existing communities became extremely limited. Internal development proceeded apace, however, with the consolidation and extension of the system of elected assemblies

The Ishráqí family, among over 200 Bahá'ís executed in Iran in the 1980s

(including an elected national spiritual assembly from 1934); the settlement of Bahá'í pioneer teachers in towns and villages throughout Iran as well as in a number of other countries, particularly in the Middle East; and the furtherance of Bahá'í community goals, including the development of a comprehensive system of religious instruction for Bahá'í youth, the collection and reproduction of Bahá'í scripture and other literature and the attainment of literacy by almost all Bahá'í women.

There is as yet little systematic research on the social composition of the Bahá'í Faith in Iran, but it would appear that the community as a whole tended towards an upward social mobility during this time, in part as a consequence of the high value that Bahá'ís place on literacy, modern education and the advancement of women.

The fall of the Shah and the establishment of the Islamic Republic in 1979 ushered in a period of massive persecution for the Bahá'ís. Within a few years, over 200 Bahá'ís had been

	NSAs	LSAs	Localities
1928	9	102	579
1935	10	135	1,034
1944	7	482	1,880
1953	12	670	2,700
1963	56	4,437	14,437
1977	123	17,415	77, 451
1992	165	20,435	120,046
1995	173	n/a	n/a

Notes: The 1928 figure for LSAs includes 5 in Germany, undifferentiated in the 1928 directory but assumed to have existed at that time (see the 1930 directory, *Bahá'í World*, vol. III, pp. 218, 222), and 17 for Iran, which represents the total number of 'administrative divisions' rather than of LSAs, for which at that early stage of administrative development in the East figures are unobtainable.

Sources: 1928 and 1935 figures calculated from *Bahá'í World*, Vol. II, pp. 189–91 and Vol. VI, pp. 505–24; 1944–77 figures from Universal House of Justice, Department of Statistics, memorandum, 15 May 1988; 1992 figures from Universal House of Justice, *Six Year Plan*, pp. 111, 114; 1995 figures from Department of Statistics, Bahá'í World Centre.

Table 2: Selected Bahá'í administrative statistics, 1928–95

executed or murdered, and hundreds more arrested. Bahá'í properties were confiscated, graveyards and shrines destroyed and thousands of Bahá'ís were discharged from work and their children dismissed from schools and universities. In 1983, the government banned Bahá'í activities and made membership of spiritual assemblies a criminal offence. All Bahá'í institutions were disbanded and have not yet been reformed. Although varying in intensity as moderate and extremist factions within the government have vied for power, the threat to the Iranian Bahá'ís remains very real. Some 10,000 Bahá'ís have fled and been resettled in other countries, but the mass of Iranian Bahá'ís remain.

Ironically, far from destroying the Bahá'í community, the Iranian persecutions appear to have stiffened Bahá'í resolve both within Iran and elsewhere. Certainly they have led to a major increase in public awareness of the Faith worldwide and have provoked extensive sympathy and support, including from individual governments, the European Union and the UN.

The Middle East

Bahá'í expansion in North Africa and the Middle East outside Iran has always been extremely limited. During the period of Shoghi Effendi's ministry, the Egyptian Bahá'í community was very active, even in the face of anti-Bahá'í agitation. One instance of this led to the legal declaration (in 1925) that the Bahá'ís were not Muslims, a pronouncement that Shoghi Effendi seized upon as evidence of the Faith's emancipation and independence from Islam. In Iraq, meanwhile, Bahá'í activity remained constrained. The Bahá'ís were few in number and the local Shí'ís were powerful and vocal in their opposition. Their seizure of Bahá'u'lláh's house in Baghdad during the 1920s became a *cause célèbre*, in which the newly established Iraqi government defied all pressure from the League of Nations, whose mandates commission had condemned the seizure as unlawful.

Elsewhere, small groups of Iranian Bahá'í pioneers established themselves in various parts of the Arab world, but circumstances did not permit more than the most cautious teaching endeavours even in countries with more 'liberal' religious attitudes. Only in secular Turkey was open Bahá'í activity eventually possible.

The situation in most of the Arab world became more difficult for Bahá'ís in the post-World War II period, in part because of suspicions engendered by the location of their World Centre in what had now become Israel. Particularly damaging was an Egyptian presidential decree of 1960, which banned all Bahá'í activities and was followed by intermittent periods of persecution. Bahá'í activities were also banned in Iraq (1970), whilst in Morocco, several Bahá'ís were actually sentenced to death (1962), until widespread international appeals persuaded the authorities to exercise tolerance.

Central Asia and the Caucasus

In the immediate aftermath of the Russian Revolution of 1917, the Bahá'í communities in Asiatic Russia had expanded their activities and begun to teach ethnic Russians. They were opposed by the communists, however, and the Bahá'ís found themselves under increasing pressure as the new government became more stridently anti-religious in its policies. From 1928 onwards, there was a buildup of anti-Bahá'í activity, including the arrest and exile of leading Bahá'ís, the banning of their organizations, the closure of their schools and libraries, and the expropriation of the Ashkhabad Temple. There was a renewal of persecution in 1938, including mass arrests and deportations that effectively destroyed the early Bahá'í communities of Russian Central Asia and the Caucasus. The Temple was later demolished after being damaged in an earthquake.

Only following the collapse of communism in the 1990s have Bahá'í activities resumed in what are now independent republics. Success has been modest but sustained, and stable Bahá'í communities have been established, in some cases including individual survivors from the earlier period.

The West

North America

The American Bahá'ís remain the largest and most important of the Western communities. During the 1920s, a joint American and Canadian national spiritual assembly replaced the earlier Baha'i Temple Unity, and under Shoghi Effendi's guidance pioneered many of the aspects of the modern system of Bahá'í administration. Its exercise of increasingly comprehensive control over Bahá'í activities was resented by some of the more individualistically inclined Bahá'ís. By the 1930s, however, the new style of organization had gained general acceptance, and the Bahá'ís embarked on a series of teaching plans to extend and expand their community, as well as to establish Bahá'í communities in Latin America (the First Seven Year Plan, 1937–44).

After World War II, the American Bahá'ís were also directed by Shoghi Effendi to help establish new Bahá'í communities in Europe. Despite extensive activity, growth within North America remained limited, so that there were still only about 5,000 Bahá'ís by 1947. Growth in Canada increased after the establishment of an independent Bahá'í administration there in 1948, eventually coming to include a significant number of Bahá'ís of Amerindian background. The long-running project to construct a Bahá'í House of Worship in the Chicago suburb of Wilmette was finally completed in 1953.

As in other parts of the West, significant Bahá'í expansion in North America only began from the late 1960s onwards, with the attraction of large numbers of youth and minority group members, particularly African Americans from poor rural areas of the southern states. These large-scale conversions raised the total number of Bahá'ís to over 100,000 by the early 1970s, and subsequent growth may have come close to doubling that figure. Given that in previous years the American Bahá'í community was predominantly middle class and white, both these influxes had a major impact on cultural and administrative style, leading for example to a much greater emphasis on music and other performing arts, and to a relaxation of the requirement that those wanting to join the community have high levels of knowledge about the Faith. More diversity was introduced during the 1980s with the large influx of Iranian Bahá'í refugees.

Europe

Although Bahá'í communities were established in Britain, France and Germany from the turn of the century, they remained extremely small. National spiritual assemblies were formed in Britain and Germany in 1923, and in 1925 an International Bahá'í Bureau was established in Geneva, which provided both a Bahá'í 'presence' at the League of Nations and some measure of co-ordination for European Bahá'í activities. Association with the Esperanto movement and the teaching tours of the American Bahá'í lecturer Martha Root led to the Bahá'í Faith becoming better known in many parts of the Continent. Root was able to attract the dowager Queen Marie of Romania to the Faith, and Lydia Zamenhof, the daughter of the Esperanto movement's founder, also became a Bahá'í. Until the Nazi regime came to power in 1933, Germany was the most active centre, but the Faith was subsequently banned there because of its 'international and pacifist teachings'. Thereafter, Bahá'í activities in most of Europe ceased during the horrific disruptions of World War II. The one exception to this was Britain, where there seems to have been little Bahá'í activity until the 1930s, but an increasing range of accomplishments from then onwards, including the adoption of an American-style teaching plan in 1944, when the war was still at its height.

After the war, American assistance ensured a rapid resumption and extension of Bahá'í activity in Western continental Europe. The German Bahá'í administration was re-established in 1946–7, and during the Ten Year Crusade (1953–63), new Bahá'í national assemblies were established throughout most of Western Europe. The British Bahá'ís, meanwhile, were directed by Shoghi Effendi towards a more global role, and successfully co-ordinated a two-year project to establish the Faith in sub-Saharan Africa

(1951–3). London also became the burial place of Shoghi Effendi, following his death there in 1957, and was later the site of the first international Bahá'í congress, held to celebrate the completion of the Ten Year Crusade and the election of the Universal House of Justice in 1963. A Bahá'í House of Worship was opened in Frankfurt, Germany, in 1964.

As in North America, larger-scale growth in Europe only started from the late 1960s, again involving significant numbers of new Bahá'ís in their teens and early twenties, and presumably reflecting developments in the increasingly independent youth culture throughout the West. The actual numbers involved were quite low, however: from approximately 1,400 Bahá'ís in 1952 to perhaps 17,000 by the early 1970s and 25,000 by the late 1980s (Smith, 'Bahá'í Faith in the West'). The question of why growth of the Bahá'í Faith in most of Europe has been so much slower than in North America remains unanswered.

The Bahá'í history of Eastern Europe has been very different from that of the West. There were Bahá'ís in European Russia during the time of 'Abdu'l-Bahá, but their activities came to a stop after the imposition of communist rule in 1917. Again, there was some Bahá'í activity in parts of Eastern Europe during the 1920s and 1930s, but this could not be resumed after World War II and the establishment of communist regimes; in any case, there were very few Bahá'ís. This all changed dramatically following the collapse of communism in most of these countries in 1989–91, and since then Bahá'í communities have rapidly developed in almost all the states of Eastern Europe, the Balkans and the former Soviet Union. The only exceptions are some parts of the war-torn former Yugoslavia. Most of these new Bahá'í communities are quite small, but two – those of Albania and Romania – have experienced such rapid growth as to make them the largest in the whole of Europe.

The Anglo-Pacific

Bahá'í activities in Australia and New Zealand began in the early 1920s. Early growth was extremely limited, despite a flurry of activities during the 1930s, including the establishment of a joint national spiritual assembly in 1934. As late as 1951, there were still only 400 Bahá'ís. Despite their low numbers, they were directed to help open the island groups of the Pacific to the Faith during the Ten Year Crusade. A Bahá'í House of Worship for the Pacific region was dedicated near Sydney in 1961. As in North America and Western Europe, more rapid growth, spearheaded by youth, began from the late 1960s, and by the late 1980s Bahá'í numbers had increased to perhaps 10,000.

The Bahá'í 'Third World'

Much of the expansion that has so transformed the Bahá'í Faith into a genuinely global religion from its position in the 1950s has been in the Third World: sub-Saharan Africa, monsoon Asia, Latin America and the Caribbean, and the Pacific Islands. These areas – along with Eastern Asia, which has a rather different Bahá'í history – also represent a 'third world' of Bahá'í expansion, after the religion's 'first world' of its Islamic heartland and its second of the West.

Like the West, there has been a common pattern of development for much of this region, with sustained growth only beginning during the Ten Year Crusade and the discovery of effective ways of presenting the Faith to the rural population. In those areas in which teaching had occurred prior to this – notably South Asia and Latin America – it had tended to be directed towards educated urban social groups, using such techniques as public lectures and the distribution of literature. This approach automatically restricted possible contact with the poor and often illiterate rural populations who still constitute the majority of the world's peoples.

The widespread growth in the Third World has necessitated the development of new techniques to consolidate the Faith and co-ordinate the activities of large numbers of new Bahá'ís. These have included the establishment of Bahá'í teaching institutes in remote rural areas and, in Latin America, the development of Bahá'í radio stations. More recently, many Bahá'í communities have initiated literacy programmes as part of an increasing emphasis on socio-economic development. Although not confined to Third World countries, Bahá'í development activities are likely to have a more marked impact in such areas, given the relative poverty and lack of resources of many such countries. The situation varies greatly from one country to another, but there has been a general emphasis on developing human capacity – for example through self-help schemes – rather than in the investment of scarce financial resources. Particular emphasis has been directed towards literacy training, education and the advancement of women, but in several countries Bahá'í medical work has also been important, receiving praise from government officials. Also significant has been the emphasis on indigenous culture and the availability of Bahá'í development resources to people of all religions, and not just Bahá'ís.

Asia

Outside the Middle East and Central Asia, here regarded as part of the 'Islamic heartland' of the Faith, Asia can be divided into Southern, South-Eastern and Eastern cultural regions, each with its own distinctive Bahá'í history.

South Asia The first and also the most important of these has been

South Asia, with Bahá'í activity in what was then British India dating from the 1870s. Early Bahá'í teaching activity was directed largely towards the educated, urban élite and middle classes, and the community remained small, even after the adoption of a more organized approach to teaching. A national spiritual assembly was established in 1923, but there was little growth. A series of systematic teaching plans on the American model was embarked upon from 1938 onwards. These led to a marked increase in the number of local assemblies in the newly independent and separate states of India and Pakistan: from five in 1939 to a combined total of twenty-eight in 1949, but the total number of Bahá'ís remained insignificant in relation to the sub-continent's vast population.

It was not until 1960–1 that effective contact was first made with the rural population in India. Thereafter growth was rapid. In 1961, there were still fewer than a thousand Bahá'ís – in a country with a population then of 439 million people – but by 1970, Bahá'í numbers had risen to over 300,000, many of the new believers being drawn from scheduled caste and tribal groups in central and northern India. This new approach to teaching was later extended to other parts of India, and there were further increases in numbers, so that the total Bahá'í population may now be approaching two million. This makes India the largest single Bahá'í community in the world, with about two-fifths of the world Bahá'í population. The logistical challenge posed by this increase has led to the pioneering development of a third level of Bahá'í administration, with elected state councils taking over much of the work formerly performed by the national spiritual assembly.

This enormous influx of new Bahá'ís has radically transformed the religious culture of the Indian community, with a remoulding of Muslim cultural elements to more Hinduized forms:

even on occasion changing the title 'Bahá'u'lláh' to 'Bhagwan Bahá'. Hindu forms are also evident in the recently completed New Delhi House of Worship (1986), built in the form of an opening lotus.

Growth in the other countries of South Asia has been far more modest. Quite large communities have developed in Pakistan and Bangladesh, both predominantly Muslim countries, but many of the Bahá'ís are drawn from the Hindu minorities.

South-East Asia The Bahá'í Faith was first established in Burma in the 1870s, the members of one village later converting almost *in toto*. A strong, active community soon developed, forging unique links with the Bahá'í World Centre by providing the marble sarcophagus that was used to house the Báb's remains. Growth was limited, however, the Bahá'ís being mostly of Muslim background in a Buddhist-majority country. Since Burma's Bahá'í linkages were with India until 1959, the community did not form a bridgehead to expansion elsewhere in the region.

There were Bahá'í visitors to other parts of South-East Asia as early as the 1880s, but it was not until the late 1940s and early 1950s that there was any permanent settlement of pioneers (mostly from India and Iran) and the beginning of sustained teaching endeavour. A network of groups and assemblies was soon established in much of the region, more rapid growth commencing in several countries from the 1950s onwards. Of early importance here was the mass conversion of several thousand tribal peoples on the Indonesian Mentawai Islands, but along with other international organizations, the Bahá'í Faith was subsequently banned (1962) and Bahá'í activities in the country ceased.

Another area of early rapid growth was South Vietnam, where the number of Bahá'ís rose to some 40,000 by 1966 and to almost 200,000 by 1975, the year of the communist takeover. In

1976, the Bahá'í Faith was banned as part of the new government's stringent anti-religious policy. Leading Bahá'ís were also persecuted. Bahá'í activities have recently been allowed to resume, but only in extremely limited form. It has not yet been possible to attempt to reintegrate the former community. The Philippines and Malaysia also experienced sustained growth (the latter concentrated among the Indian, Iban and Chinese peoples), and now have sizeable communities.

East Asia The first Bahá'ís to live in China were Iranian merchants in Shanghai, one as early as the 1860s, but Bahá'í activity there only seems to have started in 1914. This was also the year in which two American Bahá'ís from Hawaii first arrived in Japan. The results of these efforts were extremely meagre, and even as late as 1933, Bahá'ís were living in only eight localities (two with local assemblies) in the whole of East Asia, mostly in Japan. A prolonged period of war and disruption followed. Bahá'í activities in Japan resumed in 1945, aided by the settlement of American and Iranian pioneers, but growth was (and remains) extremely modest.

Activities in South Korea and Taiwan began in the 1950s, and later in Hong Kong and Macao, all with moderate success. By contrast, the anti-religious policies of the communist governments in the People's Republic of China, North Korea and Mongolia prevented Bahá'í expansion in these areas. Following recent political changes, however, a Bahá'í community has been established in Mongolia and there is now a scattering of Bahá'ís in China.

Sub-Saharan Africa

It was not until the 1950s that there was any sustained Bahá'í expansion in sub-Saharan Africa. Bahá'í groups had earlier been established in South Africa (c.1912) and Ethiopia (1930s), and there were isolated Bahá'ís in several other countries, but overall there had been little development. This changed rapidly following the start of the two-year Africa Project (1951–3) launched by Shoghi Effendi and co-ordinated by the British Bahá'ís. By 1953, pioneers from various countries had opened fourteen territories, seventeen local spiritual assemblies had been formed, and translations of Bahá'í literature had been made into a number of languages.

Progress during the Ten Year Crusade was even more marked, and by 1963, there were probably more than 50,000 Bahá'ís in the whole continent and over a thousand local assemblies had been established. Four regional assemblies serving enormous areas were formed in 1956 as an overall administrative framework. The pattern of expansion was uneven, with Uganda initially the area of most rapid growth. Accordingly, it was Uganda that Shoghi Effendi designated as the location for both the first African international conference (1953) and the construction of the 'mother' House of Worship for the continent at Kampala (dedicated in 1961).

Except for Zaire (then the Congo), growth was at first largely confined to the British territories, where the prevalence of English and less stringent immigration regulations made pioneer settlement easier. Some of the greatest progress occurred in those areas where indigenous Africans took the lead in expansion activities, however, and in a continent then dominated by European colonialism, the early emergence of African Bahá'í leaders was a particularly important development. The areas experiencing the greatest difficulties were those under Portuguese rule, where the Bahá'ís faced systematic persecution. In what is now Guinea-Bissau, this led to to the death of the first African Bahá'í martyr (1966).

Since the 1960s (when most African countries became

independent), significant progress has continued in many areas, such that there are now probably over a million African Bahá'ís (about one-fifth of the world total). The situation is extremely varied, however, not only in terms of numbers – Nigeria, Cameroon, the Central African Republic, Chad, Zaire, Kenya, Rwanda, Uganda, Malawi, Zambia and Zimbabwe all having significant Bahá'í populations – but also in terms of the strength and administrative effectiveness of the individual national Bahá'í communities (now nearly all with their own national spiritual assemblies). In several countries, there have been Bahá'í medical, educational or development projects, which in some cases have attracted favourable attention from governments; but in other countries, political or religious restrictions on Bahá'í activity or civil strife (as in Liberia) have impeded growth.

Latin America and the Caribbean

Bahá'í activity in Latin America began soon after World War I with the arrival of two American Bahá'í women, Martha Root, who made an extensive tour of the region in 1919, and Leonora Holsapple (Armstrong), who settled in the Brazilian city of Bahia (Salvador) in 1921. There was no sustained support from the North American Bahá'í community until the 1930s, however, and Bahá'í expansion only really began with the first Seven Year Plan (1937–44). Under Shoghi Effendi's direction, pioneers settled in all the independent republics, teaching commenced, and by 1943 a total of nineteen local assemblies had been established. In 1945, the first Latin American Bahá'í congress was held in Panama, and in 1947 administrative direction was passed from the North American to the Latin American Bahá'ís, with the formation of two regional teaching committees, one for South

America and one for Central America and the Antilles. The committees were replaced by two elected assemblies in 1951, and in 1961 twenty-one independent national assemblies came into existence.

Although the new Bahá'í groups were often extremely active – with programmes of public meetings, translation and publication, radio broadcasts, children's classes and the like – growth was limited. Activities were generally North American in style and largely directed towards the urban, educated minority. This situation started to change dramatically when contact began to be made with the generally poor, rural and often illiterate native Amerindian population. This involved bridging a marked cultural divide. The first breakthrough occurred in Bolivia in 1956, where the community rapidly grew to some 8,000 Bahá'ís with ninety-eight local spiritual assemblies by 1963. Similar breakthroughs occurred in Panama (c.1961), where Bahá'ís from the small Amerindian minority soon came to form a large proportion of the Bahá'í community, and eventually in most other countries with Amerindian minorities. In Brazil, with its greater ethnic diversity, 'mass teaching' from the 1970s onwards led to a comparable expansion, so that along with Bolivia, Peru, Ecuador, Colombia and Venezuela, it now has one of the largest Latin American Bahá'í communities. All told, there are now probably three-quarters of a million Bahá'ís in the region (some sixteen per cent of the world's total).

The region's first House of Worship was opened in Panama in 1972. Also of note has been the pioneering role of Latin America in developing Bahá'í radio stations since 1973, used as a means of informing scattered rural populations about the Bahá'í teachings as well as promoting indigenous culture. Amerindian Bahá'í cultural troupes have also performed widely outside Latin America.

The situation in the Caribbean has been somewhat different. Most of the islands are small and until recently remained under colonial rule. Bahá'í expansion was at first extremely limited, and it was not until the 1960s that sustained activity began in many countries, with independent national spiritual assemblies being established mostly in the 1970s and 1980s. The total number of Bahá'ís still remains small, but given the often tiny size of the host populations, they represent a significant minority in several countries. The exception to the general pattern has been Cuba, where government restrictions have impeded growth.

The Pacific

Except for the 'Anglo-Pacific' (Australia, New Zealand and Hawaii, see above), there was effectively no Bahá'í activity here until the Ten Year Crusade, when pioneers settled in many of the island groups. A regional assembly was established in 1959. Growth was at first generally slow, and there was bitter opposition to Bahá'í activities by some of the Christian Churches on several islands, leading in some instances to actual persecution. Many communities then experienced rapid expansion, so that now a number of countries have Bahá'í minorities of over five and even ten per cent of the total population. Although constituting only a small minority of the world's Bahá'í population (less than two per cent excluding Australia and New Zealand), the Pacific represents one of the most important areas of Bahá'í expansion. It is also of note that the only head of state in the world who is a Bahá'í is Malietoa Tanumafili II of Western Samoa. This is also the site of the first Bahá'í House of Worship in the region outside Australia (opened in 1984).

Conclusion

From messianic Shí'ism to a world religion

In reviewing the history of the Bábí and Bahá'í religions, a number of themes are evident. Basic to these is the transformation described by Shoghi Effendi, whereby 'a heterodox and seemingly negligible offshoot of the Shaykhí school of the Ithná-'Asharíyyih sect of Shí'ah Islam' became a 'world religion' (*God Passes By* xii).

It is, indeed, quite astonishing that a movement so deeply embedded in nineteenth-century Iranian Shí'í esotericism and messianic expectation as Bábism was should have given birth to the Bahá'í Faith, a religion that has now gained followers from virtually every religious tradition and nation in the world.

In trying to understand this development, a number of points may be made:

1) The Bábí religion clearly carried a tremendous religious charge. In the six years of the Báb's ministry, Iranian religious life was convulsed, and even after his execution his followers continued in their fervour and their willingness to die for their Faith. Even though Bábism was destroyed as a cohesive movement, its remaining adherents became a strong foundation for the subsequent growth of the Bahá'í Faith.

2) Bahá'u'lláh's own impact was extremely potent. He was able both to resurrect the dispirited, divided and despised remnant of the Bábís as a religious community, and subsequently to transform them into a new creation of his own. He was also able to infuse his followers with an essentially world-embracing vision that enabled them to take his message and teachings to individuals

and groups outside the conceptual world of Iranian Shí'ism.

3) The first key development in the transformation of the Bahá'í Faith into a genuinely international movement was the establishment of Bahá'í groups in the USA and other countries in the West. This involved the elaboration of new expressions of Bahá'í beliefs, a process that involved both 'Abdu'l-Bahá and the new Western Bahá'ís.

4) There was a subsequent worldwide expansion of the Faith, which while small in scale added greatly to the diversity of its membership.

5) A second key development was the beginning of larger scale recruitment of new Bahá'ís from the 1950s, a continuing process of transformation whereby the Bahá'í Faith began to assume the form of a world religion. This growth has been concentrated in – but not confined to – the so-called Third World, and has again involved significant new elaborations of Bahá'í belief and practice, including a far greater emphasis on issues of social transformation.

6) The overall process of transformation – 'from messianic Shí'ism to a world religion' – has featured a series of geo-cultural 'breakthroughs', by which progressively more ethnically and socially diverse people have become Bahá'ís, as well as the development of a wider range of elaborations of Bahá'u'lláh's original message.

Charisma, organization and the Covenant
Alongside this first transformation has been a second. Clearly the attraction that the Báb and Bahá'u'lláh held for their followers as well as the authority they possessed were sufficiently extraordinary for them to become the centres of dynamic religious movements. Yet for a religion to survive, more is needed than simply the charisma of its founders. It must maintain its cohesion and strength even in the face of opposition from the wider society, and also from one generation to the next, despite disputes

over the succession of leadership and changes in the social environment. This the Bábí movement was unable to do.

By contrast, the Bahá'í Faith has proved remarkably successful in maintaining its unity and dynamism despite continuing persecution in the land of its birth, internal challenges to each of its successive leaders, and encounters with an increasing range of social environments. Again, several factors may be noted here:

1) From the time of Bahá'u'lláh onwards there has been a concern with the development of effective organizational forms. Given that for the whole period of his ministry Bahá'u'lláh lived in exile, in areas increasingly remote from the mass of his followers, this was essential. Communications had to be maintained with Iran and some system had eventually to be developed so that the Iranian Bahá'ís could organize their affairs without constant reference to Bahá'u'lláh about every matter of detail.

2) With the international expansion of the Bahá'í Faith during the ministries of 'Abdu'l-Bahá and Shoghi Effendi, and the need for co-ordination of widely scattered Bahá'í groups in several continents, effective organization became even more essential.

3) The need for a reliable system of communications was met by the establishment of a courier system and a secretariat, the latter the precursor of the extended administrative apparatus of the contemporary Bahá'í World Centre.

4) The need for localized forms of administration was met by the development of the system of spiritual assemblies (local and later national). These provided the Bahá'ís with a relatively flexible system whereby they could administer their own affairs in accordance with locally perceived situations and requirements.

5) The growth of the system of assemblies greatly reduced the importance of clerically trained Bahá'ís who had initially exercised a leadership role within Iran. The appointment of Hands of the Cause, and later of other 'institutions of the learned', continued

the Islamic concept of the 'ulamá, but in limited form, with executive authority clearly resting with the elected assemblies.

6) The succession of centres of the Faith at first embodied
the traditional Islamic pattern of inherited religious leadership,
with 'Abdu'l-Bahá and Shoghi Effendi – as the first in a line of
projected Guardians – occupying roles in some ways directly
analogous to those of the Shí'í Imáms. As with Shí'í faith in the
Imáms, there was great stress on the importance of divinely
ordained designation of the line of succession, this achieving
doctrinal form in the Bahá'í doctrine of the Covenant.

7) The Covenant doctrine gave each successive centre of
the Faith what sociologists would term 'charismatic legitimacy',
that is the appointed centres were each believed to possess
divine authority – undoubtedly a factor in the lack of success of
those Bahá'ís who disputed their authority.

8) At the same time, there has been a progressive shift from
personalistic to more bureaucratic forms of leadership, the importance of the person of 'Abdu'l-Bahá as a continuing religious focus
contrasting markedly with the emphasis on the institution of the
Universal House of Justice as a body transcending its individual
members.

Major religious motifs
In addition to these two major processes of transformation, there
has been a more complex series of developments in Bábí and
Bahá'í doctrine and practice. There is obviously a marked contrast
between the Bábí movement and the contemporary Bahá'í Faith in
terms of major religious concerns: Bábism formed a heterodox
part of a Shí'í conceptual world that is very distant from most of
us. Nevertheless, Bábism also came to form the seed-bed for the
future emergence of the Bahá'í Faith, and there are important
points of continuity. In reviewing these contrasts and continuities,

it is useful to follow the development of a number of major themes that appear central to the Bábí and Bahá'í religions:

1) The crucial element of continuity appears to be the belief that there is or should be a source of divine guidance to which human beings give their allegiance and devotion. The first two Shaykhí masters appear to have occupied such a role for their followers, and the search for a new master was clearly a factor in the first emergence of the Bábí movement. Again, the early Bábís may have had differing theological conceptions as to the Báb's 'station', but they were united in recognizing him as being in some way God's representative in the world. When cut off from him by his exile, and later by his death, the Bábís turned to others, seeking a further source of guidance. By a combination of his personality, his teachings and writings, and his organizational skills, Bahá'u'lláh offered a new point of unity, and in a remarkably short time, the vast majority of the Bábís had recognized him as their Lord. Thereafter, the successive centres of the Faith – supported by some form of designation and by the Covenant doctrine – readily gained the allegiance of the mass of the Bahá'ís. The lack of success of those who came to be designated as 'Covenant-breakers' is noteworthy in this regard.

2) A second major theme is millenarian expectation, although this has taken quite different forms at various stages of Bábí–Bahá'í history. A significant part of the initial appeal and impact of the Bábí movement came from its expression of Shí'í messianism. However, when the Báb laid explicit claim to be the Mahdí, it was in a way that diverged strongly from literalistic traditional belief. The Báb also introduced the new messianic figure of 'He whom God shall make manifest', a prophetic expectation that defined the Bábís' later acceptance of Bahá'u'lláh. Bahá'u'lláh and his successors referred to the present as a new age of millenarian fulfilment, but they also taught that the working out of the new world of the resurrection would be through an ongoing evolutionary process. They distinguished

between the establishment of a more just and peaceful world (the 'Lesser Peace') in the near future and the spiritualized world of the more distant future (the 'Most Great Peace'), and referred to events such as World War I in apocalyptic terms. Millenarianism became a vision of future bliss and an encouragement to Bahá'í striving.

3) The Bahá'í concept of the future millennium has also become linked with a specific programme of social reform and transformation. This does not have any real antecedent in the Bábí movement, but first took its distinctive form in the social and political teachings advanced by Bahá'u'lláh in 'Akká. This theme has received increasingly strong emphasis in recent years.

4) Another complex theme is that of divine law. The early Bábís were scrupulous in their observance of Islamic law, and both the Báb and Bahá'u'lláh announced their own legal provisions to replace the Islamic *sharí'a*. The laws of the *Bayán* never really became operative, but those of the *Aqdas* form the basis for contemporary Bahá'í law. In obvious contrast to the Islamic legal system, Bahá'í law has received little elaboration, and at present rests mostly on individual conscience rather than social pressure for its observance. Although the Hands of the Cause, Counsellors and Auxiliary Board members are all regarded as institutions of 'the learned', they are not comparable to the Islamic 'ulamá.

5) One major Bábí theme was the concern with esoteric knowledge. Shaykhism formed part of the rich tradition of Islamic esotericism, and this was also strongly expressed in Bábism, with its emphasis on numerology and talismans and its use of veiled and highly symbolic language. There are traces of this in some of Bahá'u'lláh's writings, but it is not a major theme. Both 'Abdu'l-Bahá and Shoghi Effendi were categorical in their rejection of Western occultism.

6) Corresponding to this decline of esotericism as an approach to religious knowledge is the Bahá'í emphasis on rationality and scientific thinking as part of a religious world-

view. This was emphasized most explicitly by 'Abdu'l-Bahá.

7) Another change relates to the accessibility of religious grace. The Bábís were very conscious of the division between themselves as true believers and the mass of Shí'ís who were unbelievers. Bahá'u'lláh, by contrast, emphasized the need for tolerance and love towards the followers of all religions, and pointed to the difficulties that even the devout might have in attaining the spiritual and moral qualities of true belief. He also stressed that his message was truly universal and not confined to those of Muslim background.

8) As to the actions required to establish the future millennial order, Bábism followed traditional Islamic conceptions and at a theoretical level advocated jihád (holy war) as the means of attainment, although in practice no such jihád was ever called. Bahá'u'lláh's position was radically different: all ideas of holy wars were rejected and the Bahá'ís were summoned to devote themselves to the peaceful teaching of their religion.

9) The Bábís also continued the traditional Shí'í regard for sacrificial martyrdom. This gave them a potent base for their own fervent heroism that so awed their opponents. Bahá'u'lláh greatly praised the station of the martyr, but encouraged his followers to live rather than die for their faith if that was possible. Up to the present time, Iranian Bahá'ís have had to face severe persecution and the possibility of martyrdom, and this has been a factor in sustaining their dedication.

The future

As to the future, the following comments may be in order:

1) It is now just over a hundred years since Bahá'u'lláh's passing (and 150 years since the declaration of the Báb). During this time, the religion he originated has endured various crises and attacks both in the land of its birth and elsewhere. It has become well established in a varied range of countries and has

succeeded in achieving an impressive global diffusion. It seems likely that this process of expansion will continue and that the Bahá'í Faith will become well rooted in a larger number of places.

2) Expansion will lead to a wider cultural diversity of Bahá'í expression, including more systematic attempts to relate the Bahá'í teachings to religious traditions outside the Islamic and Judeo-Christian ones. Non-Islamic and non-Western forms will also become increasingly prominent within the Bahá'í world. (For an impression of the diversity that already pertains, the reader should watch the video coverage of the New York Bahá'í Congress in 1992.)

3) Almost certainly, present attempts to extirpate the Faith in Iran will fail, albeit that the Bahá'ís within Iran are likely to remain a beleaguered minority in the immediate future. The Iranian Bahá'í diaspora will remain a vital part of the Bahá'í world community, but it will become increasingly diverse, as its members become more firmly part of their various 'host' cultures.

4) The overall structure of Bahá'í administration now seems well established. There will probably be a tendency towards decentralization in some national Bahá'í communities, and the Indian precedent of intermediate state councils is likely to be copied in a number of the larger ones. New specialized agencies will no doubt be established to deal with particular issues and needs.

5) Concern with issues linked to social transformation and the development of Bahá'í community life will increase. In this regard, ties with non-Bahá'í organizations with similar objectives, such as those linked to the United Nations, will also increase.

6) Finally, given that the Bahá'í Faith is becoming increasingly widespread and that it claims quite specifically to be a global religion with answers to contemporary world problems, we may expect both the Bahá'í teachings and the Bahá'í community to come under more serious study by those outside the Faith.

Chronology of Important Dates

1844	The Báb's declaration of mission to Mullá Husayn (22/3 May) and pilgrimage to Mecca (September–July 1845).
1845	Trial of the Báb's emissary in Iraq (13 January). The Báb returns to Shíráz (July).
1846	The Báb escapes from Shíráz (23 September) and proceeds to Isfahán.
1847	The Báb is transferred from Isfahán to Mákú (March–July). Táhirih returns to Iran (spring–summer). Mullá Muhammad Taqí Baraghání is murdered (late October).
1848	The Báb is transferred to the fortress of Chihríq (April–May) and later tried in Tabríz (July). The Conference of Badasht (June). The death of Muhammad Sháh (4 September). The conflict at Shaykh Tabarsí (10 October–10 May 1849).
1850	Seven leading Bábís in Tehran are executed (19/20 February). Conflicts in Nayríz (27 May–21 June) and Zanján (c.13 May–January 1851). The execution of the Báb (8/9 July).
1852	The attempt on the life of the Shah (15 August). Bahá'u'lláh is imprisoned in the Black Pit.
1853	Bahá'u'lláh is exiled to Iraq. Further conflict in Nayríz (October–December?).
1854	Bahá'u'lláh withdraws to the mountains of Kurdistán (April–March 1856).
1856–63	Bahá'u'lláh's increasing pre-eminence within the Bábí community. Composition of the *Hidden Words* (1858) and *Íqán* (1862).
1863	Bahá'u'lláh leaves Baghdad. In the Ridván garden (22 April–3 May). He journeys to Istanbul and Edirne.
1866	Separation of the Bahá'ís and Azalís in Edirne. Bahá'u'lláh's claims are promulgated among the Bábís in Iran.

1868	Bahá'u'lláh is arrested and exiled to 'Akká (August). Azal is sent to Famagusta.
1870s	First Bahá'í missionary goes to India.
c.1873	Bahá'u'lláh's book of laws, the *Kitáb-i-Aqdas*.
1875	'Abdu'l-Bahá's *The Secret of Divine Civilization*.
1877	Bahá'u'lláh moves out of the city of 'Akká.
1889	Russian authorities arrest Shí'í murderers of a Bahá'í.
1892	Death of Bahá'u'lláh (29 May). Succession of 'Abdu'l-Bahá.
1894	Beginning of Bahá'í missionary activity in North America.
1908	'Abdu'l-Bahá released from Ottoman confinement and moves to Haifa (1909).
1910–13	'Abdu'l-Bahá journeys to Egypt; Europe (August–December 1911); and North America and Europe (March 1912 to June 1913).
1914	Bahá'í activity begins in Japan.
1921	Death of 'Abdu'l-Bahá (28 November).
1922	Shoghi Effendi publicly named as Guardian (January). His first letter on Bahá'í administration is sent to the West. Process of administrative consolidation begins.
1928	Suppression of the Bahá'í communities of Soviet Asia begins.
1934	Bahá'í schools in Iran closed. Purge of Bahá'ís in government employment.
1937–44	First American Seven Year Plan. Systematic planning becomes part of Bahá'í activity. The Bahá'í Faith is banned in Nazi Germany.
1948	Establishment of the 'Bahá'í International Community' affiliated with the United Nations. Construction of the superstructure of the shrine of the Báb begins (–1953).
1951	Formation of the International Bahá'í Council and Shoghi Effendi's first appointment of Hands of the Cause.
1953–63	Ten Year Crusade. Bahá'í House of Worship in Wilmette completed.
1957	Death of Shoghi Effendi in London (4 November). The Hands assume supreme authority.
late 1950s/ early 1960s	Beginning of large-scale conversions in Latin America, Africa and South and South-East Asia.

1960 on	Bahá'í activities in Egypt banned.
1963	Establishment of the Universal House of Justice. First Bahá'í world congress in London.
1967	Permanent BIC office established in New York.
1968	Establishment of the Continental Boards of Counsellors.
1973	Establishment of the International Teaching Centre. First Bahá'í radio station opens in Latin America.
1979	Islamic revolution in Iran. Major persecution of the Bahá'ís begins.
1983	Seat of the Universal House of Justice comes into use. Office of Social and Economic Development established.
1985	The Universal House of Justice issues its statement on peace, *The Promise of World Peace*.
1992	Second Bahá'í world congress, held in New York. Publication of the *Kitáb-i-Aqdas*.

Further Reading

Recent years have seen a rapid growth of scholarly studies of Bábí and Bahá'í history, but the field is essentially still in its infancy: very much remains to be done.

A general overview of Bábí–Bahá'í history is provided by the present author's *The Babi and Baha'i Religions: From Messianic Shí'ism to a World Religion*, which also gives a detailed guide to further reading. For an extensive listing of publications see William P. Collins, *Bibliography of English-Language Works on the Bábí and Bahá'í Faiths, 1844–1985*. Shoghi Effendi's *God Passes By* is a forceful account of Bábí and Bahá'í history up to the 1940s by the Guardian of the Faith.

The Bábí movement has received the most attention from scholars. The most recent studies are those by Abbas Amanat, *Resurrection and Renewal: The Making of the Babi Movement in Iran, 1844–1850*; Hasan M. Balyuzi, *The Báb: The Herald of the Day of Days*; B. Todd Lawson, 'The Qur'an commentary of Sayyid 'Alí Muhammad Shírází, the Báb'; Denis MacEoin, 'From Shaykhism to Bábism: A study in charismatic renewal in Shí'í Islam'; and idem. *The Sources for Early Bábí Doctrine and History: A Survey*. Important source materials include 'Abdu'l-Bahá, *A Traveller's Narrative Written to Illustrate the Episode of the Báb*, trans. Edward G. Browne; Khan Bahadur Agha Mirza Muhammad, 'Some new notes on Bábism'; and Nabíl, *The Dawn-Breakers*. See also Peter Smith and Moojan Momen, 'The Bábí movement: A resource mobilization perspective'. Some passages of the Báb's writings have been translated into English in *Selections from the Writings of the Báb*.

There is as yet only one study devoted specifically to the life of Bahá'u'lláh, H. M. Balyuzi's *Bahá'u'lláh: The King of Glory*. See also the same author's *Eminent Bahá'ís in the Time of Bahá'u'lláh*. An important recent study is Juan R. I. Cole, 'Iranian millenarianism and democratic thought in the 19th century'. There are translations of several of Bahá'u'lláh's writings, including: *The Hidden Words of Bahá'u'lláh; The Kitáb-i-Aqdas: The Most Holy Book; The Kitáb-i-Íqán: The Book of Certitude; Prayers and Meditations of Bahá'u'lláh; The Proclamation of Bahá'u'lláh to the Kings and Leaders of the World; The Seven Valleys and the Four Valleys;* and *Tablets of Bahá'u'lláh Revealed After the Kitáb-i-Aqdas*.

On the life of 'Abdu'l-Bahá see H. M. Balyuzi, *'Abdu'l-Bahá: The Centre of the Covenant of Bahá'u'lláh*. Translations of his writings include: *The Secret of Divine Civilization; Selections from the Writings of 'Abdu'l-Bahá; The Tablets of the Divine Plan;* and *The Will and Testament of 'Abdu'l-Bahá*.

The main study of Shoghi Effendi's life and works is by his widow: Rúhíyyih Rabbání, *The Priceless Pearl*. Shoghi Effendi's English-language writings include: *The Advent of Divine Justice; The Faith of Bahá'u'lláh, A World Religion; Messages to the Bahá'í World, 1950–1957; The Promised Day is Come;* and *The World Order of Bahá'u'lláh*.

The writings of the Universal House of Justice include: *The Constitution of the Universal House of Justice; The Promise of World Peace;* and *Wellspring of Guidance: Messages from the Universal House of Justice, 1963–1968*.

On overall developments in the Bahá'í Faith since the 1950s see Peter Smith and Moojan Momen, 'The Bahá'í Faith 1957–1988: A survey of contemporary developments'. An invaluable source of information for developments from the mid-1920s onwards is the successive volumes of *Bahá'í World*. An impression of cultural diversity within the Bahá'í community at the present time can be gained from the five-video set of the Bahá'í World Congress, New York, 1992.

Bibliography

'Abdu'l-Bahá. *The Secret of Divine Civilization*. Trans. Marzieh Gail. 3rd edn. Wilmette, Ill.: Bahá'í Publishing Trust, 1979.
— *Selections from the Writings of 'Abdu'l-Bahá*. Trans. Marzieh Gail et al. Haifa: Bahá'í World Centre, 1978.
— *The Tablets of the Divine Plan*. Rev. edn. Wilmette, Il.: Bahá'í Publishing Trust, 1977.
— *A Traveller's Narrative Written to Illustrate the Episode of the Báb*. Trans. Edward G. Browne. 2 vols. Cambridge: Cambridge University Press, 1891.
— *The Will and Testament of 'Abdu'l-Bahá*. Wilmette, Ill.: Bahá'í Publishing Committee, 1944.
Amanat, Abbas. *Resurrection and Renewal: The Making of the Babi Movement in Iran, 1844–1850*. Ithaca, NY: Cornell University Press, 1989.
Bahá'í World, The (Bahá'í Yearbook), vols. I–XII. Wilmette, Ill.: Bahá'í Publishing Trust, 1926–56; vols. XIII–XVIII. Haifa: Bahá'í World Centre, 1970–86.
Bahá'u'lláh. *The Hidden Words of Bahá'u'lláh*. Trans. Shoghi Effendi. Oxford: Oneworld Publications, 1986.
— *The Kitáb-i-Aqdas: The Most Holy Book*. Haifa: Bahá'í World Centre, 1992.
— *The Kitáb-i-Íqán: The Book of Certitude*. Trans. Shoghi Effendi. 3rd edn. London: Bahá'í Publishing Trust, 1982.
— *The Proclamation of Bahá'u'lláh to the Kings and Leaders of the World*. Haifa: Bahá'í World Centre, 1967.
— *The Seven Valleys and the Four Valleys*. Trans. Ali Kuli Khan and Marzieh Gail. Oxford: Oneworld Publications, 1992.
— *Tablets of Bahá'u'lláh Revealed After the Kitáb-i-Aqdas*. Trans. Habib Taherzadeh et al. Haifa: Bahá'í World Centre, 1978.
Balyuzi, H. M. *'Abdu'l-Bahá: The Centre of the Covenant of Bahá'u'lláh*. London: George Ronald, 1971.
— *The Báb: The Herald of the Day of Days*. Oxford: George Ronald, 1973.
— *Bahá'u'lláh: The King of Glory*. Oxford: George Ronald, 1980.
— *Edward Granville Browne and the Bahá'í Faith*. London: George Ronald, 1970.
— *Eminent Bahá'ís in the Time of Bahá'u'lláh*. Oxford: George Ronald, 1985.
Cole, Juan R. I. 'Iranian millenarianism and democratic thought in the 19th century.' *International Journal of Middle East Studies*, vol. 24 (1992), pp. 1–26.
Collins, William P. *Bibliography of English-Language Works on the Bábí and Bahá'í Faiths, 1844–1985*. Oxford: George Ronald, 1990.
Lawson, B. Todd. 'The Qur'an commentary of Sayyid 'Ali Muhammad Shirazi, the Bab.' Ph.D. dissertation. McGill University, 1987.

MacEoin, Denis. 'From Shaykhism to Bábism: A study in charismatic renewal in Shí'i Islam.' Ph.D. dissertation. University of Cambridge, 1979.
– *The Sources for Early Bábí Doctrine and History: A Survey.* Leiden: Brill, 1992.
Momen, Moojan. *The Bábí and Bahá'í Religions, 1844–1944: Some Contemporary Western Accounts.* Oxford: George Ronald, 1981.
– *An Introduction to Shi'i Islam: The History and Doctrine of Twelver Shi'ism.* New Haven, CT: Yale University Press, 1985.
Muhammad, Khan Bahadur Agha Mirza. 'Some new notes on Bábism.' *Journal of the Royal Asiatic Society,* July 1927, pp. 442–70.
Nabíl (-i-A'zam). *The Dawn-Breakers: Nabíl's Narrative of the Early Days of the Bahá'í Revelation.* Trans. Shoghi Effendi. Wilmette, Ill.: Bahá'í Publishing Trust, 1932.
Rabbání, Rúhíyyih. *The Priceless Pearl.* London: Bahá'í Publishing Trust, 1969.
Shoghi Effendi. *The Advent of Divine Justice.* Rev. edn. Wilmette, Ill.: Bahá'í Publishing Trust, 1963.
– *The Faith of Bahá'u'lláh, A World Religion.* Wilmette, Ill.: Bahá'í Publishing Trust, 1959.
– *God Passes By.* Rev. edn. Wilmette, Ill.: Bahá'í Publishing Trust, 1974.
– *Messages to the Bahá'í World, 1950–1957.* 2nd edn. Wilmette, Ill.: Bahá'í Publishing Trust, 1971.
– *The Promised Day is Come.* Rev. edn. Wilmette, Ill.: Bahá'í Publishing Trust, 1980.
– *The World Order of Bahá'u'lláh.* Rev. edn. Wilmette, Ill.: Bahá'í Publishing Trust, 1965.
Smith, Peter. *The Babi and Baha'i Religions: From Messianic Shí'ism to a World Religion.* Cambridge: Cambridge University Press, 1987.
– *The Bahá'í Religion: A Short Introduction to its History and Teachings.* Oxford: George Ronald, 1988.
– 'The Bahá'í Faith in the West: History and social composition.' In *The Bahá'í Faith in the West,* ed. Peter Smith. Los Angeles, CA: Kalimat Press, forthcoming.
– 'Expansion and distribution of the Baha'i Faith.' Unpublished paper.
– 'A note on Babi and Baha'i numbers in Iran.' *Iranian Studies,* 17: pp. 295–301.
Smith, Peter and Moojan Momen. 'The Bábí movement: A resource mobilization perspective.' In *In Iran,* ed. Peter Smith, pp. 33–93. Los Angeles, CA: Kalimat Press, 1986.
– 'The Baha'i Faith 1957–1988: A survey of contemporary developments.' *Religion,* vol. 19 (1989), pp. 63–91.
Universal House of Justice, The. *The Constitution of the Universal House of Justice.* Haifa: Bahá'í World Centre, 1972.
– *The Promise of World Peace.* Oxford: Oneworld Publications, 1986.
– *Wellspring of Guidance: Messages from the Universal House of Justice, 1963–1968.* Wilmette, Ill.: Bahá'í Publishing Trust, 1969.

Index